T.L. Osborn

God's LOVE Plan

THE AWESOME DISCOVERY

BOOKS BY THE OSBORNS

BELIEVERS IN ACTION—*Apostolic–Rejuvenating*

BIBLICAL HEALING—*Seven Miracle Keys*
4 Visions–Over 60 years of Proof

CHAOS OF MIRACLES
Christ's Historic & Supernatural Visitation to the DRC

FIVE CHOICES FOR WOMEN WHO WIN
21st Century Options

GIVE THANKS—*Reflections on Christ's Redemption*

GOD'S BIG PICTURE—*An Impelling Gospel Classic*

GOD'S LIFE IN YOU—*52 Facts*
Discover God's Purpose in You

GOD'S LOVE PLAN—*The Awesome Discovery*

HEALING THE SICK—*A Living Classic*

JESUS & WOMEN—*Big Questions Answered*

JESUS IS TOUCHING SOSHANGUVE
God's Love Revealed in South Africa

LIFE–TRIUMPH OVER TRAGEDY (WHY)
A True Story of Life After Death

MIRACLES-PROOF of God's Love

NEW LIFE FOR WOMEN—*Reality Refocused*

NEW MIRACLE LIFE NOW—*For Asia and The World*
A Global Communiqué of The Christian Faith

OUR WITNESS—*Proof of the Resurrection*

PEACE IS A LIFESTYLE—*Truths for Crisis Times*

SOULWINNING—*Outside The Sanctuary*
A Classic on Biblical Christianity & Human Dignity

THE BEST OF LIFE—*Seven Energizing Dynamics*

THE GOOD LIFE—*A Mini-Bible School–1,519 Ref.*

THE GOSPEL ACCORDING TO T.L. & DAISY
Their Life & World Ministry–510 pg. Pictorial

THE MESSAGE THAT WORKS
T.L.'s Revealing Manifesto on Biblical Faith

THE POWER OF POSITIVE DESIRE
An Invigorating Faith Perspective

THE WOMAN BELIEVER—*Awareness of God's Design*

UNKNOWN BUT NOT FORGOTTEN
The Gospel Reaches Parakou, Benin

WOMAN WITHOUT LIMITS
Unmuzzled—Unfettered—Unimpeded

WOMEN & SELF-ESTEEM—*Divine Royalty Unrestrained*

YOU ARE GOD'S BEST—*Transforming Life Discoveries*

USA HQ:

OSBORN MINISTRIES INT'L

P.O. Box 10, Tulsa, OK 74102 USA

T.L. & Daisy Osborn, Co-Founders

LaDonna Osborn, CEO

Tel: 918/743-6231

E-Mail: ministry@osborn.org www.osborn.org

Canada: Box 281, Adelaide St. Post Sta., Toronto M5C 2J4

England: Box 148, Birmingham B3 2LG

(A Registered Charity)

Bible quotations in this book may be personalized, paraphrased, abridged or conformed to the *person* and *tense* of their context in order to foster clarity and individual application. Various language translations and versions have been considered. Biblical references enable the reader to compare the passages with his or her own Bible.

The Author

ISBN 978-0-87943-093-1

Printed in the USA 2016-09

CONTENTS

DEDICATED

TO THE PURPOSE of ministering love in a hurting world, with Bible assurance that God values people, that He is not mad at them, and that the price He has paid for them is the proof of their worth.

T.L. Osborn

YOU ARE made for life, not for death.

You are made for health, not for disease.

You are made for success, not for failure.

God wants no one to live without sight, or to be alone without friends, or to be unhappy.

His love is in action now.

He wants no one to live in shame, or fear, or disgrace.

He paid a big price for you which proves your worth to Him.

LaDonna Osborn

INTRODUCTION

God's Greatest Idea

LOVE IS THE GREATEST idea ever to come from God to human beings. There is *faith and hope and love, but the greatest of these is love.*[1Co.13:13]

The Bible says: *God is love.*[1Jo.4:8] God created you, so you are the product of love.

That means that you are made for love. You are not made for hate or fear.

You are made for life, not for death.

You are made for health, not for disease.

You are made for success, not for failure.

You are made for good things, not for bad things.

God loves you so much that He paid a big price to have you near Him, the price of His Son.

When Jesus Christ came to this earth, everything He did underscored how much God values people.

Love in Action

Jesus passed near a blind beggar by the name of Bartimaeus.

The blind man cried out, *Jesus, have mercy on me!* The crowd told him to be quiet, but *when Jesus heard him, He stopped there in the road and said, Tell him to come here.*[Mar.10:46-52LB]

Jesus is interested in people. He came to help us. He wants no one to live without sight or to be alone without friends or to be unhappy.

Bartimaeus jumped up and came to Jesus. What do you want me to do for you? Jesus asked. I want to see! the blind man said. And Jesus said, All right, it's done! Your faith has healed you. And instantly the blind man could see, and followed Jesus down the road! [Mar.10:46-52LB] That is love in action.

In my parents' crusade in the Democratic Republic of Congo (then known as Zaire), two blind women were healed. What a love gift from God.

Throughout the night they danced in the streets of Lubumbashi, telling the people about their healing miracle.

The good news about God's big love-plan is that this Jesus is unchanged today. He wants to do for you whatever you need or desire Him to do.

The Healing Power of Love

One day a leper came to Jesus. The disciples said, *Get him away. He is unclean.* But Jesus said: *No, let him come. He has faith.* [Mar.1:40-42]

You see, the purpose of Christ's coming was to help people, to save and to bless them. Love caused our Lord to reach out His hand and touch that leper and his flesh was instantly healed.

He is reaching out to you, as you read this book. His love-plan is to do whatever is necessary to lift you to total happiness, health and success.

Across the town of Kisumu, Kenya a leper woman called Miriam Gare, crawled on the ground to attend the Osborn crusade. Her fingers and her feet were gone. She carried her belongings in a basket on the back of her head as she crawled.

She heard about Jesus and believed on Him the first time she heard my father teach God's love-plan. Christ came to her and Miriam got up on those stumps of legs and began walking and weeping and thanking God because she was miraculously cured. She became active in the local church whose pastor took a personal interest in her. She became a radiant witness of Jesus Christ and of His love in action.

God Is Never Mad at You

They brought a prostitute to Jesus one day. Self-righteous people said, *Let's stone her to death. She is an unclean woman.*[Joh.8:3-11]

But Jesus said: *Wait a minute. God did not send his Son into the world to condemn the world, but to save the world.*[Joh.3:17] You see, He values each human person.

He forgave her sins, made her pure and clean again and restored her self-dignity and self-esteem as a lady.

Jesus does not want to accuse or judge or condemn you. His value of you is so great that He seeks to lift and bless you, to help you become all that your Father created you to be.

In one of my parents' crusades, a young woman, who had lived by prostitution since she was a teenager, attended and heard them teaching God's big love-plan.

She came because she had a large cancerous tumor in her uterus. She was a terminal case, rejected by society, not even thirty years old.

She discovered that God loved her and valued her and He was not mad at her. She heard them teaching that God loved her so much that even during all the years that she had lived in prostitution, He had kept on loving her and had never given up on her.

She wept as she learned that Jesus Christ had come to this world on her behalf and had already assumed all of the guilt, condemnation and judgment of all of her sins. She understood that Jesus had already suffered the penalty that she herself deserved; that He had done it in order to redeem her and to restore her to God as though she had never committed a wrong deed.

God Already Did His Part

That young woman understood for the first time that Jesus Christ had already endured the penalty for and judgment of her sins. Therefore, they could never be legally punished the second time. Since Jesus suffered her punishment she was no longer guilty.

She learned that the cross of Jesus proved several things: 1) That she was valued by God. 2) That she was loved by God. 3) That her sins had already been punished. 4) That God cared for her even before she knew about Him. 5) That God had already redeemed her and that all she had to do was to hear about His love-plan, believe it and accept it.

That woman trusted in what Jesus did on her behalf. She accepted Him and she was saved.

Instantly, as she was thanking God for His love, the big tumor disappeared. It was a miracle. She was totally healed. She received peace with God. He had come home to live in her. She had come home to God and her body responded to the power of God's life at work in her. The cancer could not stay.

You see, God's love-plan is to restore people. He never destroys anyone—not their health, not their happiness, not their reputation, certainly not their self-esteem.

God wants to do good things for you today. His love is in action now. He wants to do for you whatever you need or desire, if you will only believe in His love-plan.

Transforming Power

As Jesus climbed out of a boat one day, a wild man came running from among the tombs. Night and day this poor creature screamed and cut himself with sharp stones. He was tormented and possessed by demons.

Jesus spoke to the evil spirits and they came out of the man and he was healed.[Mar.5:2-8,15]

That is what Christ came for. He never wants a human person to live in shame or fear or disgrace. He values people—every person, and He will do whatever you need in order to develop your finest potential as a God-person, successful, happy, healthy and valued.

A young man was brought to one of the Osborn crusades who had been attending a medical college, studying to become a doctor. For some reason his mind snapped, and he became insane. His classmates took straps of iron and bound his hands and feet, then chained him so he could not escape because he was a menace even to himself. They took him back to his village, where his family kept him strapped, chained and locked in a hut with a door made of crossed poles, wired together, to allow ventilation.

His food was tossed to him like one would feed a dangerous animal. He would lunge at people and try to bite them as they passed his hut. Someone had kicked him in the mouth and knocked his front teeth out.

Four men brought him to the crusade, with his ankles and wrists bound with the chained iron cuffs. They also gagged him to prevent his biting someone. Jesus came to that man while we were teaching God's love-plan to the multitude. The demon spirits that had tormented him went out of him and he became perfectly normal.

They removed the gag from his mouth and took the chained bands off his legs and arms. There were thick callouses on his wrists and ankles, caused by the iron bands.

He resumed his studies at the university and became a living witness of God's big love-plan which we are sharing with you in this book.

You Were Created for Love

Why does God love you so much? Why did Jesus give His life for you? Why did He die in your place? Why did He send such a wonderful plan to you through this book?

He values you.

You were created by love. God paid a big price for you, which proves your worth to Him.

The first proof that God has chosen to reach out to you is already evident: This book is in your hands. Whatever you need or desire from God has already begun.

As you continue to read, God's big love-plan will become more clear and real to you. As that happens, you will discover the secrets which will open to you a new lifestyle of happiness, health, prosperity and self-worth.

The key is in your hand right now. As you turn the next pages, you will discover how to take control of your life, and how to relate yourself to the rich and happy lifestyle God created you for.

LaDonna Osborn,
D.Min.

INTRODUCTION

JESUS CHRIST is not a religion, but a person.

Why evangelize Hindus, Buddhists, Moslems?

Is life without purpose? Does it lead to nothingness?

If there is a God...can I ask questions?

I have the feeling that there is hope for me.

Chapter I

Purpose Out Of Confusion

A FRENCH TEACHER spending her vacation in America, visited our offices in Tulsa, Oklahoma.

Since she spoke practically no English the receptionist called our French translator to host the lady.

As the impact of our world ministry hit her, she began to pose questions about our *programme d'évangélisation, religion et doctrine.*

Our translator took advantage of the questions to witness about Christ. She explained the simplicity of what we teach. It is Jesus, not a religion, but a person—the Son of God who assumed the guilt of our sins and suffered the judgment we deserved in order to free us from all guilt and to restore us to God as though we had never sinned.

To the French lady, this seemed almost too simple to be real. Her questions: "Why evangelize people of other lands such as Hindus, Buddhists,

Moslems? They are content in their religions. Why do we believe ours is better?

"How can we be sure that God exists? That Jesus is His Son, or that He was born of a virgin? Why was His death any different than that of any other person? Or His blood any more divine than that of anyone else? Why are we so convinced that He was raised from the dead?

"Doesn't it seem that life is without purpose and leads to final nothingness? Why do we believe that the Bible is true?"

Should We Ask Questions?

Then, of course, to reassure her hostess that she was not a pagan: "You know, I have my religion. I feel it's important for children to receive their 'first communion.' After all, we aren't savages! But anyone who thinks or reads or has average intelligence, must ask questions. You see, I'm a divorcee with two children to raise. I wonder about them without a father, to face an uncertain future. Why not just end it, once and for all?

"But if there is a God, and if He is good, why does He permit so much misery and sickness? Why are innocent children born with defects, crippled, etc.? If God can do miracles, why does He not cure everyone?

"Probably there is a devil; that would explain a lot of things...but original sin by Adam and Eve?

Isn't that the problem of sexual relations between men and women? The Bible talks of a tree whose fruit was forbidden. It says that Adam and Eve chose to disobey God and ate of that forbidden fruit. Consequently, sin and evil and suffering are the result. I suppose that's logical.

"But, if I simply followed your counsel and welcomed Jesus into my heart and trusted Him to guide me and live in me day after day, what are the prayers I should recite? What are the sins I should abstain from? To just receive Jesus, as I am, and believe that He comes and lives in me, is that all? It seems so simple. I think one should first improve oneself. As a divorcee, am I automatically out of the church? Can I be helped?

"You are saying that I, in my predicament can know God and relate to Him as a friend. As a Father. And He will help me.

"Are you sure? Why has no one told me this before? I've been confused for many years.

"Every time anyone talks to me about religion, I get the impression that they want to enlist me in something, in their church or their denomination. But you've talked to me without clichés and religious bigotry. I have the feeling that there is hope for me, that Jesus is the way, that the gospel is put in true perspective, and that my own life now has purpose."

She left with a newly discovered life-pattern in Jesus Christ. The New Testament would be her guide. Some of our books given to her by our translator, fortified the decision she had made to follow Jesus.

She had discovered God's big love-plan.

PURPOSE OUT OF CONFUSION

IS IT POSSIBLE to find the right road in life?

Why so much religion with so little reality?

What causes loneliness, depression and suicide?

Has religion made God too mysterious?

The business world believes in solving problems. Am I sacrilegious if I want to solve my problems about God?

Chapter 2

Good, Big, Loving, Powerful

THE WHOLE WORLD is searching for purpose in living, the reality of God, evidence that the Bible is true—and if so, how to make a practical application of it in an individual life.

Why is the cross of Christ so important and what does it mean today? Why the constant guilt of sin and wrong doing? What is the way to really find peace with God? Is it possible to find the right road in life? Is there an answer?

If God is good and if He created human persons, why are the minds of people so often confused? Why is there so much fear, loneliness and guilt?

If God is the Creator, what is the reason for so much poverty and want in this world? Why so much prayer without response? Why so much religion with so little reality? Why so much knowledge with so few answers?

What causes loneliness, depression and suicide?

Why is there so much war? Family division? Divorce? Violence? Brutality?

Why do people not keep the Ten Commandments?

Can what the Bible calls **salvation** be a practical experience? Can a person be changed? Is God interested in human persons? Does He want us to have health, happiness, success and prosperity in this life?

Poverty, Sickness and Problems

Must a person live in poverty to have true humility and to be close to God? Can sickness and pain be the will of our heavenly Father when earthly parents would never desire that their children be diseased?

Has religious tradition programmed society to believe that God is complex and mysterious? Does a limited concept of God prevent people from enjoying the happiness, health and success He intends for them?

The business world believes in solving its problems. But if there is a problem in one's relationship with God, or if logical questions are posed, that can be regarded as sacrilegious. The average person usually ignores spiritual questions and continues toward an uncertain future, to face an unknown God with concepts that contradict human logic. Must life be blindly committed to fate?

Millions have abandoned the idea of faith in God, relegating Him and the Bible to nothing more than medieval delusions.

I have written this book to help you see God as good and as big and as loving and as powerful as the Bible says He is. *For God is good, and he loves goodness.*[Psa.11:7LB] *There is nothing but goodness in him.*[Psa.92:15LB] *There is nothing too hard for him.*[Lev.32:17]

LET'S RELATE God to human needs and not limit Him to church sanctuaries.

We have witnessed abundant proof that God is real, that Jesus Christ is alive.

We discovered that His miracles are contained in the seeds of His promises—and we can plant them.

Chapter 3

We Want To Tell Everybody

FOR OVER FIVE decades, my wife, Daisy, and I have preached about the miracles and love of God to multitudes of from twenty to three hundred thousand people. We've proven, thousands of times, that God is what He says He is; that He will do what He says He will do; that the Bible is real and that what it says is true.

The Christian religion is bogged down in theological complexities. Society has almost relegated God and miracles to legend and superstition.

Instead of relating God and faith to people and their needs, many relate Him only to church sanctuaries.

We have witnessed abundant proof that God is real, that Jesus Christ is alive, and that His miracle-working power is unchanged today. Wherever His promises can be planted in receptive hearts and minds, they produce wonders in human lives.

We see God at work every time we see cancers healed, paralytics walk, blind and deaf people restored, every time we see unhappy lives transformed, or defeated poverty-level families discover God's abundant living and prosperity. We see the miracle of His seeds reproducing of their kind in the lives of those who believe in Him.

Let's Sit Down and Talk

When Daisy and I went to India as missionaries, we were very young. We wanted to share God's big love-plan with those who had not yet heard about Him. We had not yet learned the secrets of simple faith in God, so there were no miracles to give proof of what we taught.

But as a result of this experience, our own lives were transformed. The Lord Jesus Christ appeared to me in our bedroom. That experience made me know that He is more than a religion, that He is alive. The Bible became a living book.

We discovered the principles of God's love-plan and how His miracles are all contained in the seeds of the promises He has given us to plant in human lives.

We have been reliving the gospels of Christ during most of our lives.

Every day our mail contains exciting testimonies of miracles and of changed lives that come to us from all over the world. It makes us want to tell everybody about God's big love-plan.

We love people. We live to help people discover their self-value and their unique value to God.

We have witnessed such wonderful miracles of His love, that we simply cannot keep silent. That is the reason for this book.

People write to us about their problems and hurts, about their struggles and sicknesses, about their needs and difficulties or problems.

We want to say to them—and to you: Let's sit down and talk. Let us share some of God's principles with you. Let us show you how you can become more than you ever dreamed, how you can be healed and blessed, how you can succeed and prosper and have God as your partner in life.

When you hear God's promises and believe them, you will be planting His miracle seeds in your life. They will produce what they say.

You are going to find yourself right in the middle of God's big love-plan of abundant living. You will look up one of these days, and discover a harvest of good things growing up all around you. Expect it and get ready to experience a new lifestyle, with God as your comrade and personal friend.

HE HATED protestant Christians, ambushed them, robbed them and even helped to kill them.

He said, "I am the one they should have crucified."

No sin can be held against anyone who believes in Jesus Christ. No Judgment will ever have to be faced.

Chapter 4

No Longer Guilty

A TROUBLED MAN attended one of our crusades in Latin America. From his youth, he hated protestant Christians. His pleasure was to steal from them or to destroy their crops or business or property. He and his friends would ambush them in the countryside, take their belongings and often beat them. He delighted in persecuting them and he told us that he even helped to kill some of them.

Jesus Christ had become real to his wife soon after they were married. Quite often their relations had been strained because of religious conflict. For nineteen years she had prayed that her husband would have a personal encounter with the Lord.

The man attended our crusade the night I talked about the way Christ suffered in our place and how He was crucified to pay the penalty for our sins.

For the first time in his life, that man realized that God created human persons to walk and talk with Him in the garden of His presence; that we are made in God's own image and since God is love, it is His big love-plan that we share His love; that hatred, evil and murder are from Satan who caused humanity to sin against God in the beginning.

He had not realized that sin was the barrier between him and God, nor that God longed for fellowship with each person so much that He gave His only Son to restore them to Himself.

The death of Christ suddenly became a reality to the man.

You Are Already Forgiven

He told us, "As I began to think about my hatred and the brutal things I had done against innocent people, I realized that every evil deed I had committed helped nail Jesus to the cross. I visualized Him hanging there between two thieves, enduring the punishment of my sins so that I would not be held guilty before God.

"As you taught, you made me realize that I was the one who should have been crucified, because I was the one who had committed evil. Jesus was innocent. He was perfect.

"I found myself weeping. I wanted to cry out, 'Why You, Lord? Why are You being crucified?

What evil did You ever do? I was the one they should have crucified! I am the guilty one!' "

That dear man rushed to the front of the big arena as soon as I invited people to express their faith in Christ. His devoted wife stood beside him as this persecutor of Christians fell to his knees and accepted forgiveness for all of his sins.

He had felt deep guilt and remorse. Now it was all gone and he realized that God held none of his sins against him.

Your Debt Is Wiped Out

The word "forgiven" means "to grant relief from payment of a debt or obligation." Jesus Christ paid our debt for us. The penalty of our sins is paid in full, like a debt that has been paid off.

Jesus assumed our guilt and suffered the full penalty of our sins, in our name, in our place.

The entire debt against the one who believes on Christ is wiped out. There is absolutely no sin which can be held against anyone who believes in Jesus Christ. Such a person shall never have to face God's judgment for sin. Jesus did that, in our name, when He suffered the judgment of our sins in His death for us on the cross.

Jesus said, *I say emphatically that anyone who believes in God who sent me has eternal life. And will never be damned* (or condemned or judged) *for his or her sins, but has already passed out of death into life.*[Joh.5:24LB]

There is now no condemnation to those who are in Christ Jesus,[Rom.8:1] *for who shall accuse those whom God has chosen? God himself declares them not guilty! Can anyone, then, condemn them?...Jesus Christ is the one who died* (for them)...*who then can separate us from the love of Christ?* [Rom.8:33-35TEV]

As far as the east is from the west, so far has he removed our transgressions from us.[Psa.103:12]

God's big love-plan provides the way for us to be restored to God as though no sin had ever been committed.

NO LONGER GUILTY

HE HAD intimate sexual relations with the girls of his neighborhood.

His problems were compounded.

The discovery of good news changed everything, including arthritis, cancer and the plight of a child born paralyzed.

The price of depression is too high. The power of the big love-plan works.

Chapter 5

He Proved God's Love-Plan

A MAN ATTENDED one of our meetings who illustrates God's big love-plan as well as anyone I know about.

He had been born in a very poor home and was uneducated.

As he struggled in life, he began, as a young man, to steal. Then he began to have intimate sexual relations with the girls of his neighborhood. He used them, and if they resisted him, he abused them. Then shame and guilt began to cloud his life.

Finally, he married one of the girls. But he was not satisfied. He continued his promiscuous lifestyle and soon he was the victim of a venereal disease. A little baby was born to his marriage, but its legs were not normal. They never moved or developed.

Guilt depressed him. He knew that he had been responsible for bringing disease to his wife, that it had now affected his child.

As he tried to conceal his guilt by drinking, he developed ulcers, then cirrhosis of the liver, and before long, cancer.

The Price of Depression

There was little food on the table. Tensions mounted. Nerves were on edge. Then the man's joints began to tighten as the pressures of life intensified. Before long, he could not lift his arms. His legs were painful when he tried to walk. Then he was obliged to use crutches.

Unemployed, afraid, resentful, guilt-stricken and angry, he hated himself—and he hated God.

In that despondent state, he heard of the crusade where we were teaching the gospel. At first, he presumed that we were foreign soothsayers or charlatans deceiving the people.

But then he asked himself, "What can I lose?"

So he hobbled to our public meeting on his crutches.

His wife accompanied him, carrying their little crippled boy in her arms.

There they listened as we taught God's big love-plan, the gospel, to that field of people.

We did not know about his case in particular. But God's love-plan had the answer which that father and his family needed.

As I taught, I explained how God created Adam and Eve well and happy, healthy and tranquil, with love and peace, with abundance and with purpose.

As that man stood there on his crutches looking at his little boy who could not walk, he thought to himself: "My wife and I have none of that. We fight and hate each other. We are sick. We have little food. We are poor. We are fearful. We are lonely. We are angry."

The Beginning of Problems

Then I explained how Satan came and caused Adam and Eve to doubt God's word, and as a result, they lost their right to God's blessings and were separated from Him.

I explained how that from that point, Adam and Eve became lonely and unhappy as they tried to live without God in their lives. Hate, lust and envy filled their lives. Problems evolved. Nervous tensions mounted. Sicknesses developed in their bodies. Finally they faced death, without God.

This man thought to himself, "That's why we are lonely. That's why I am in trouble. That's why my little boy cannot walk. That's why I am about to die of cancer. That's why my body is filled with pain. That's why I am full of remorse. That's why my wife and I are nervous. We are out of touch with God. Our sins have separated us from Him."

Love Never Gives Up

Then I explained about God's big love-plan. I quoted the Bible verse that says *God is love.*[1Jo.4:8] I explained that God's love never gives up on us.

I quoted the Bible scripture that says, *God is not willing that* ***any*** *should perish, but that* ***all*** *should come to repentance,*[2Pe.3:9] and the verse that says, *God so loved the world that he gave his only begotten Son, that whoever believes in him would not perish, but would have everlasting life.*[Joh.3:16]

I emphasized the verse in Romans 1:16 which says, *The gospel* (the good news) *is the power of God.*

What is the gospel?

It is good news.

What good news?

I told that crowd that night what the good news is. That man and his wife listened.

It is the good news of what Jesus Christ did for each one of us when He died, as our substitute, in our name, on the cross.

Good News for Whom?

I explained who the good news is for.

It is good news for **each one who has sinned.** Jesus bore our sins so that we do not have to bear them, but be forgiven and receive His peace.

Good news for **each one who is sick.** Jesus bore our sicknesses so that we do not have to suffer diseases and sicknesses, but be healed of them and receive His health.

Good news for **each one who lives with guilt.** He bore our guilt so that we can receive His pardon and salvation and be as innocent and blameless as though we had never sinned.

Good news for **each one who is condemned** by the penalty of sin. Jesus bore our condemnation and offers His forgiveness and freedom from condemnation forever.

Good news for **each one who is poor.** Jesus bore our poverty in order to share with us His riches.

Good news for **each one who has failed.**

You see, this man was a failure. I did not know his circumstances or that he was there, any more than I know about you, but God knew. So I explained: Jesus bore our failures in order to live in us and to share with us His success.

Good news for **each one who is affected** by an incurable disease. Jesus bore our diseases and suffered our death, so that He could give us His life.

That man nudged his wife, and said, "That's the answer. That explains Christ's death. That's the gospel I never knew about. That's not just a religion. That affects us and our problems."

Then he thought to himself, "This must be too good for me. I am too far gone. My heart is too sinful. I am too sick. My child was born this way. Nothing can help us. We are without hope."

But I kept teaching. I emphasized that *the gospel is the power of God to everyone who believes.*[Rom.1:16]

Believes what? Believes that what Jesus did on the cross, we do not have to do.

I reminded the crowd that Jesus said, *If you can only believe, ALL things are possible.*[Mar.9:23]

Tough Questions for a Tough Decision

Out there on that field that man asked himself, "Can I believe in this love-plan? Is it too good to be true for me? Did Jesus take my place?"

"Jesus was a good man. I have been a terrible person. I have wronged so many people. My life has been so destructive. Did Jesus Christ take my place? Did He suffer for my sins? Did He take my diseases, even this cancer, this arthritis?"

He wrestled with his own logic.

He reasoned within himself:

"I know what brought on this cancer. It was my lifestyle, my rebellion. Did Jesus suffer that for me? Jesus was too good to do that."

I kept emphasizing: *The gospel is the power that brings salvation to* ***everyone*** *who believes.*Rom.1:16 "Only believe," I said. *All things are possible if you can only believe.*Mar.9:23

Then I explained: You must realize that God's big love-plan, includes healing, and forgiveness, and blessing, and abundance—everything that Jesus died to provide—everything that you can possibly need or desire from God.

And as I kept teaching, that man decided, "I will believe what Mr. Osborn is saying. I do believe it." When I finished my lesson, then I helped all who wanted to pray to God, by leading them in a prayer.

He repeated the prayer, and as he did, he could not restrain his tears. He confessed all of his wrong doing to God. The reality of His love engulfed him. Peace and joy came to his life.

He and his wife found themselves weeping together, embracing each other.

The Healing Power of Love

They were in each other's arms, when suddenly he thought of his little son. He told his wife, "Put him down, honey. I believe his legs are changed. Put him down."

The little boy was perfectly whole. His little legs functioned and had become strong for the first time in his life. They instantly became normal by the miracle of God's love.

Then he noticed that he did not have pains in his shoulders. His crutches were not hurting him. There was no pain in his knees.

He dropped his crutches aside and discovered that while he had received peace and joy in his spirit, the Lord had healed his arthritis.

He and his wife brought their little boy to the platform. The little boy was whole. There was absolutely no paralysis. They were overwhelmed with joy and gratitude to God for such a big love-plan.

The family walked home together. Their house was now a new home, where peace had come to reign.

The happy mother fixed some food. It smelled good to the father. Then he realized that his stomach had no pain. The suffering from stomach ulcers was not there. And his side felt good too. There was no swelling in his liver.

He ate. There was no pain. He pounded his side. His liver did not hurt him. The cancer was obviously gone. The ulcers were healed. He was a new man physically, mentally and spiritually.

The Fruits of Friendliness

He began to tell people about God's love for him.

His personality became pleasant and friendly.

The Bible says, *If any one is in Christ, that person is a new creature. Old things are passed away; all things are become new.*[2Co.5:17]

He began to express his friendliness to people. He no longer accused and swore at people. He was no longer cynical or sarcastic. He could smile at people.

A businessman observed him and offered him a job. He did good at the job and succeeded. He was promoted in the company. His salary was raised time after time. Now he heads the company.

He is a faithful Christian. He is a product of God's big love-plan.

GOD PROVED how much He esteems you by the price He paid for you.

You can hook up with God in a personal encounter that will mark you for life.

Five facts unlock the way to God's happy, healthy, successful lifestyle.

Chapter 6

God's Beautiful Dream

THE GREATEST THING that can happen to you is to discover your value to God and His big love-plan.

God Himself proved how much He esteems you by the price He paid for you—the price of the life of His Son. His act of love ends all argument about your worth.

Once you discover the value God places upon you, then you are ready for the most powerful and dynamic experience a human being can have.

You are ready to identify yourself with God in a personal encounter that will mark you in His big love-plan for as long as you live.

This will be the most powerful fact that I can share with you because it is what opens the gates to God's riches, health, success and abundance. God's big love-plan includes all that you can ever need or desire in life.

Here are the five facts that unlock the way to God and to His happy, successful lifestyle.

Understand:

1) Who Jesus Christ is; 2) Why He came; 3) Why He was put to death; 4) Why He came back from the dead and 5) How He lives today.

Then relate yourself to Him in a personal way because He is your open door to His love-plan.

The Plan and the Condition

To understand why Jesus Christ came, you need to understand the problem which created the barrier between God and people.

God's dream for humanity is recorded in Genesis. His plan was to reproduce Himself in a man and a woman.

Adam and Eve whom God created in His own image and likeness, were not required or forced to respect God any more than you are.

They were placed in the garden of Eden and given *every tree that is pleasant to the eye and good for food; and the tree of life also in the midst of the garden.* [Gen.2:9]

God made one single restriction to measure their faith and confidence in His dream for them. He said: *You may eat from every tree in the garden except the tree of knowing good and evil; the day you eat from it you will certainly die.* [Gen.2:16-17]

The Way to Live and Prosper

They were expected to have confidence in what God said, and that is all that He expects of you and me.

If Adam and Eve trusted in God's integrity, they would live and prosper with Him forever. If they abused His trust and disbelieved His word, the process of deterioration would begin and they would die.

Their lack of trust in the integrity of what God said was later called sin.

The simple rule that God made was *that the person who sins would die.*[Eze.18:4,20]

Later it was repeated in another way: *The wages of sin is death.*[Rom.6:23,8]

HUMANS ARE not robots.

Friendship with God depends on two-way communication.

Trust the integrity of God's plan and discover life's best.

Without mutual faith between God and people, the good life is ended. The light goes out.

When you have faith in God, you can value people and help them become all that God created them to be.

Chapter 7

Root Of The Problem

GOD WANTED THE human persons whom He had created to have total happiness, divine purpose and abundant living.

But their friendship had to be two-way. God would need to be sure that Adam and Eve cherished His company, like He cherished theirs. A one-way relationship could not constitute a friendship or a companionship.

The Bible implies that God would walk into the garden of Eden and visit with them. He could communicate with them because He had created them like Himself.

They were not robots. They were given total freedom of will. They could be God's friends or question or even reject His ideals.

God created Adam and Eve for happiness, health and abundance, but His plan was logically dependant upon mutual trust and integrity. Created in God's own image, Adam and Eve would share a common faith with God which would be the basis for their interrelations. They could count on the integrity of whatever God said. He expected to count on their will and their word. They would relate to each other on the basis of mutual confidence and trustworthiness.

God said, in essence: Trust the integrity of my plan and you'll have life's best. But if you decide not to believe what I say, then you will forfeit what I have designed for you and the process of deterioration and death will destroy you.

What Happened to the Good Life

Satan, God's enemy, heard of God's dream and conceived a scheme to induce Adam and Eve to betray God's trust and thereby destroy the foundation of His love-plan.

Satan came into the garden and spoke with Eve, urging her to eat of the forbidden tree. He deliberately contradicted God, asserting himself as the authority and said:

If you eat of that tree, ***you will not die.***[Gen.3:4] The woman was convinced. *So she ate of the fruit and gave some to her husband, and he ate too.*[Gen.3:6] Both Adam and Eve shared the same violation of the trust between them and God.

Result:

God came into the garden and, after questioning Adam and Eve, spelled out for them what the consequences would be:

There would be no grounds for a relationship with God. Adam and Eve had exercised their free wills and had, by their action, disregarded and disbelieved what God had said. They forfeited the intimate relationship that God based His big love-plan on.

Without mutual faith and trustworthiness, the relationship between God and them was abrogated. The good life was finished.

Unbelief in God is the most destructive poison with which a human person can be infected. By disavowing God's integrity, we renounce our own dignity and self-value. A sense of personal unworthiness then reflects itself outwardly toward others by criticism, accusation, condemnation, judgment and destructive, abusive relationships. These attitudes become life's norm; and all that God planned to make life beautiful, happy, healthy and prosperous—is destroyed.

When you have faith in God, you can value people and help them to become all that God created them to be, because you understand their potential as God-persons.

Lack of faith in God invariably results in a lack of self-value, which then reflects itself outwardly in a lack of appreciation of the value and the potential of others.

Though God cherished the companionship of Adam and Eve, His own integrity required that the full measure of His law be applied to their violation of His trust. Otherwise, His word could never be relied upon.

They were no longer qualified to dwell in the garden with God. Separated from His plenty and beyond His protection, they would now be subject to their new master, Satan.

When the Light Goes Out

That was the beginning of suffering, disease, pain, hate, lust, envy, murder, jealousy, loneliness, guilt, poverty, hunger, destruction and death.

Sin had entered the human race. It would be inbred into all generations to come.

*Whereas, by one person sin entered into the world, and death by sin; so death passed upon all persons, for that all have sinned.*Rom.5:12

The fundamental sin that obstructed God's companionship with humankind was not murder or adultery or lying or stealing or hatred or abuse.

It was the assumption or philosophy or attitude that God did not mean what He said.

The devastating result of unbelief in God is that when you do not trust Him, you do not trust yourself, or anyone else.

When you decide that God has no integrity, your own integrity is abandoned. Conscience is calloused. Dignity is desecrated. The human person deteriorates and dies. The light goes out.

Could that be society's problem today?

Without trust in God's integrity, human persons sink into disgrace, and despair, disease and desecration, destruction and desolation.

WHEN FAITH in God is repudiated, people lose faith in their friends and neighbors and, consequently, in themselves.

Who needs God in our industrialized world of science?

Can the ills of society be cured through the 'miracle' of psychoanalysis?

Can mental sicknesses be passed on to physical bodies and to business circumstances?

Chapter 8

Change You And Change Your World

DAISY AND I have been privileged to teach God's big love-plan to literally millions of people, face to face. Tens of thousands of lives have been enriched by new faith in God and we have watched them experience miraculous changes in nations around the world.

Science, industry or philosophy can never satisfy the heart cry of people.

When faith in God is repudiated, people lose faith in their neighbors and, consequently, in themselves. They become spiritually listless and pursue life without direction or purpose.

If people happen to be displeased or angry with themselves, unhappy or discontented, they may turn to lawlessness, destruction, murder and suicide.

Ecclesiastical orthodoxy has camouflaged the simplicity of God and His plan for life with a forbidding smokescreen of complicated liturgy, pious rituals and incantations that, to people who need God's help, seem archaic and empty.

A young Parisian collegiate asked: "Who needs a God in our industrialized world of science?" Yet our most rudimentary problems remain unsolved.

A young businessman in London quipped: "Why do people cling to religion and believe in fables called miracles? Who needs them when we have the modern genius of medical science?" Yet many ordinary illnesses such as the common cold, still cannot be cured.

A young Brussels philosophy major ridiculed faith in God as she reasoned: "We enjoy the greatest psychological discoveries humanity has ever known. We are penetrating the complexities of the human mind until the ills of society can all be cured through the miracles of psychoanalysis." And yet there is a higher rate of suicide, per capita, today than ever before in human history.

Peace for the War Inside

People are at war with themselves. Emotional and psychological disturbances destroy a greater percentage of society than ever before.

A psychiatrist at the world famous Johns Hopkins Hospital reported that sixty percent of the patients there require mental and spiritual treatment, not physical.

It is estimated that fifty to eighty-five percent of all people are passing on their mental and spiritual sicknesses to their bodies. Nothing is more poisonous to the chemistry of the human body than a negative, cynical, demoralizing mental or spiritual attitude.

A management professional who takes over faltering businesses and gets them back on their feet, estimates that ninety-five percent of the problems he encounters are not in the businesses themselves but in the persons who run them.

People get messed up in life and then transmit their own inner confusion to their business circumstances. They are disoriented inside themselves and before long, their businesses reflect their own inner ills. Get the people straightened out and their business dilemmas will soon be resolved.

Problems in marriages, in families, between neighbors and in community relationships are reflections of attitudes and thought patterns harbored and smoldering inside individuals.

It is a psychological fact that you are quick to criticize others for what you subconsciously dislike in yourself.

You are jealous only of what you desire to be yourself.

You resent in others only what you yourself tend to impose upon others.

The main problem in your home, your family, your job or in your neighborhood exists in the person you see when you look in the mirror. Get that person straightened out and you'll discover who has the power to change your world and to make it beautiful.

When your own life is in order, your husband or wife, family or neighbors will be changed as by a miracle.

HE WAS A bachelor who hated sanctimonious swindlers.

100,000 people made him curious and he heard the love-plan.

The price is already paid for anyone to receive the rich and happy lifestyle God planned for people.

When Jesus appeared to a non-believer.

A smile was the signal.

Chapter 9

He Discovered New Love

THE OWNER OF a large hotel attended our Holland crusade in The Hague. Over 100,000 people gathered nightly on the huge open field called the Malieveld. This man became curious about what was attracting so many people.

He was a bachelor who hated the idea of God. He carried a deep resentment toward the clergy whom he considered to be nothing more than sanctimonious swindlers. He despised religion and avoided any contact with Christians or churches.

During a period of war he had served as a Dutch naval officer. In battles at sea, he had watched the bodies of sailors flung through the air by the explosion of bombs. He said he had shaken his fist toward heaven many times and cursed the idea of God, daring Him, if He existed, to strike him down.

He had prided himself in the fact that he had never prayed a prayer in his life.

Then came our crusade. The enormous crowds made him curious, and he decided to attend.

That night I taught about the simplicity of prayer and of calling on the name of the Lord Jesus in order to receive God's blessings and the new life which His big love-plan guarantees.

He listened intently as I stressed the price that Jesus Christ had paid to restore us to God as though we had never sinned. I explained that Christ had given His life as a ransom for our sins in order for us to be able to receive God's immeasurable blessings.

Had Christ not died in our place, our sins would still separate us from God. But He loved us so much, and wanted to share His life with us so much that He gave His Son, who went to the cross and endured the full penalty of all of our sins so that no judgment for sin could ever be imposed upon us—not now, not in the hereafter.

The Miracle of Prayer

This man had never known about God's love-plan called the gospel. The privilege of coming to God in prayer had been disdained by him as a ceremonial ritual by theological defrauders in order to ensnare people in their religious webs. Now he began to realize that a great price had been paid so that human persons can come to

God and receive the rich and happy lifestyle which He originally planned for people.

To conclude my teaching that evening, I stressed that 1) *Whoever would call upon the name of the Lord would be saved;* Rom.10:13 2) that Jesus desires to share His life with each person; 3) that the greatest miracle of prayer is when Jesus responds and comes in to impart His miracle life to someone; and 4) that a person is literally reborn with new divine life when they receive the Lord Jesus by faith into their heart.

I then instructed the multitude in how to put their faith in God as they prepared to pray.

The man told us later: "As I looked around and saw everyone bowing their heads and getting ready to pray, I asked myself: 'Can 100,000 fellow-Hollanders all be deceived? Are they all wrong? Maybe not!' I decided that there may be something to this God after all."

Then he told us: "I said to myself, if I ever expect to pray a prayer in my life, this must be the best opportunity I will ever have. I am surrounded by 100,000 people on this field who believe in God and in prayer. I am going to do what this man says. If there is a God, He will surely answer me here where so many people believe on Him."

When Jesus Appeared to the Man

He placed his hands on his chest and closed his eyes to pray and the moment he did, he said an overwhelming consciousness of God gripped him. As this feeling of awe came over him, he said "I looked up into the heavens to pray and just as I lifted my eyes, there before me stood Jesus Christ. I was so frightened that my instinct was to want to hide myself. But His eyes were fixed on mine and I seemed riveted there. I could not budge.

"The Lord's eyes were like fire and they seemed to penetrate my being, seeing every thing I had ever done and every blasphemy I had ever spoken. In a few seconds it seemed that my whole lifetime passed before me. I knew He saw it all. Such fear and awe seized me that I felt I dare not blink an eye.

"I felt the deepest possible remorse swell up inside of me for the life I had lived and for the way I had cursed this man Jesus. Why had I hated Him so? What ever made me doubt His existence? As I looked at Him, my eyes were a fountain of tears pouring out of me. If He would only stop looking into me.

"After what seemed an interminable search of my very soul, while my eyes were riveted to His, slowly but certainly a soft and compassionate smile came across the savior's face. With that tender smile of love, I knew I was forgiven. He did not hold my debauchery and cynicism against me. He forgave me. Oh what joy. What relief. I knew I was forgiven.

"As His smile became fully visible, He faded from my sight. All of my physical strength was gone and I sank to the ground, sobbing and weeping.

"The people around me were praying to God. It seemed like heaven to me. The multitude sounded like a huge waterfall as the voices of a hundred thousand Hollanders were expressing faith in God and their love for Him.

"When I was able to get to my feet, I was a new person. I guess I was born again. Jesus was living in me. I had His new life.

"I went up to the platform and tried to tell my fellow countrymen what had happened but I could not speak because of weeping. The joy I felt was unexplainable. I was reborn."

We happened to be staying at that man's hotel during the crusade. There was a lovely open-air garden used as a breakfast court below our room. The next morning after the man's conversion, the weather was beautiful and the hotel guests were eating outside. Our windows were opened wide to let in the fresh morning air.

We could hear a man's voice above the others. He kept talking about Jesus. We looked out the window and this dear hotel owner was going from table to table, telling about his experience with Christ. He felt that everyone in his hotel should know that Jesus is alive and real. The man had experienced God's big love-plan.

What a marvel that God loves you and values you so much that He paid the full price to restore you to His beautiful family. His love-plan is so perfect that, the moment you accept it and believe it, you can come home to God and it is as though you had never sinned.

HE DISCOVERED NEW LOVE

GOD WILL NOT quit on you.

The love-plan that ended the scourge and proved your value.

The finest way to say 'Thanks' for God's best.

Jesus did it in YOUR name.

The crux of the plan that freed you from all guilt.

Chapter 10

Your Life...Paid In Full

GOD NEVER ABANDONED His love dream for you.

God never gave up on you all the time you were living in despair, without any knowledge of His big love-plan.

God is love and love never quits.

His love went into action the day Adam and Eve broke confidence with Him. He found a just and legal way to restore humankind back to an intimate relationship with Him.

His love-plan would end the scourge of death and restore people to life.

What was His love-plan and how would it restore you to God and legally absolve you from the penalty of death for your sins?

Love Had a Solution

Substitution was the legal answer. If someone who is innocent of sin would be willing to take the place of someone who is guilty and assume full punishment for their sins, then the guilty one would be free and could be restored to friendship with God as though no wrong had ever been done.

It was love's idea.

God created people to live, not to die. *God was not willing that any should perish but that ALL should come to repentance.*[2Pe.3:9]

Now you can understand why Jesus Christ came and died for you.

*God so **loved** the world that He gave his only begotten Son, that whoever believes in Him should not perish but have everlasting Life.*[Joh.3:16]

God believed that if He proved His love for you in such a costly way, and if He sent someone to tell you what He did, that you would respond and say: "That settles it. God values me just as I am. He wants me to have His best."

That is why I wrote this book. It is God's idea. I think the finest way I can show my gratitude to God for His best in my life, is to tell it to someone like you.

In order to provide for you a substitute who had no sin of his own, God gave His own Son.

Proof That the Plan Could Work

Jesus was born by a miracle conception. The Spirit of God overshadowed a virgin and the seed of divine life was created in her womb. That, in itself, is a miracle and it sounds incredible. But it was necessary because Jesus could not be born of human seed that was infected by sin, and be innocent of sin.

Not only was Christ's conception of divine seed—and therefore without the heritage of sin, but His life among people had to be sinless, in order to qualify as our substitute. God's Son must be subjected to the same temptations of sin as any human person is. He must be exactly like us and resist what human persons had not resisted. He must prove that God's original plan could work—that human persons could choose God's word, and never dishonor His integrity.

Jesus must be tempted by Satan just as Adam and Eve had been.

This is why, as soon as He was mature, Jesus was led into the wilderness where Satan came to tempt Him exactly as he had come to tempt Adam and Eve in the garden of Eden.

Every time Satan tried to bring question on God's word, Jesus rejected his suggestions and forthrightly asserted what God had said.[Mat.4:1-11]

Under the most trying circumstances, Jesus believed God's word.

The Bible says that throughout the earthly life of Christ, *He was in every respect tested as we are, yet without committing any sin.*[Heb.4:15]

Jesus Christ was perfect. He was untouched by the **seed** of sin and He **committed** no sin.

No Debt Is Paid Twice

That explains why He was able to be your substitute. Since He had no sin in Him, and committed no sin, He could assume your sins and give His life as a ransom for you.

If your penalty of death was assumed by Him, you would be legally absolved of that penalty.

Since no debt can be paid twice, or no crime punished twice, you would be restored as though no wrong had ever been done.

Since Jesus Christ suffered the penalty you and I deserved, and since He did it in our name and on our behalf, the moment we believe in His love-plan, we are no longer guilty before God and will never be judged for any sin we have ever committed.

The judgment we deserved was assumed by our substitute, in our name and in our place, and that judgment can never be imposed on us again.

This is the crux of God's big love-plan in the Bible that we call salvation.

GOD SAID the same thing 41 times in the Bible.

He has a very big heart and a very big soul.

He never afflicts and punishes people with sicknesses, suffering and poverty. He carries no whip.

God wants your life fulfilled. He wants you to develop your finest potential.

He wills only good for you.

Chapter 11

He Plans Only Good For You

I WISH THE whole world could know how good God is.

The Lord is gracious and full of compassion. [Psa.86:15;111:4;112:4;145:8] Jesus was everywhere *moved with compassion.* [Mat.9:36;14:14;18:27; Mar.1:41;6:34] *His compassions fail not.* [Lam.3:22]

Thirty-three times just in the book of Psalms, it says, *His mercy endures forever.*

For You, Lord, are good, and ready to forgive; and plenteous in mercy to all them that call upon you. [Psa.86:5]

God says, *I will rejoice over you to do you good...with my whole heart and with my whole soul.* [Jer.32:41] God has a very big heart and soul, and it all rejoices over you and me to do us good.

Many people think of God as some sort of dominating master who lords it over people with a whip in his hand to afflict and punish his children with sickness, suffering and poverty. This is not true.

God created you and me for His wonderful lifestyle and He wants us to enjoy His blessings of happiness, health, success and prosperity. That is His will for you and me today.

God created us in His own image and, therefore, human beings instinctively search for God's lifestyle, whether they admit it and are conscious of it or not.

When the Light Turns On

Around the world, whether on the busy streets of Paris, New York or Bogota; whether in village towns of the Philippines, India, China or Africa, humanity's instinctive search is for a living God. It is written all over people's faces. It is expressed in the way they walk. It is reflected in their spirits. They would give anything on earth to know that God is real, and to receive a miracle from Him. To imagine that such a God, if real and living, is interested in them individually seems beyond their imagination.

I have watched the light turn on in tens of thousands of faces when they realized that God loves them, that He is not angry at them, that He cares for each detail of their lives. It can happen to you, while reading this book.

The truth of the matter is that God wants your life to be fulfilled. He wants you to enjoy happiness and to develop your finest talents and capabilities. Your potential is God-given and limitless. God has the same pleasure in seeing you blossom and succeed as any good parent experiences when their child excels.

God is not a destroying deity who sends disease and pain.[Luk.9:56; Nah.1:7] He does not want poverty and lack at your house. He has plenty, and it is for you to enjoy.[Joe.2:26; Ecc.5:18-19; Pro.10:22; Psa.68:19;104:24; 3Jn.2]

God is never pleased by needless suffering, poverty, sickness and failure.

People, plagued by inner fears and guilts, poison their own systems and engender within themselves disease and deterioration. Young and old alike permit their lives to be eroded by the psychological traumas and chemical poison of hatred, jealousy, envy and greed.

Their lack of faith in God, in their neighbors, and in themselves makes them crumble and degenerate.

Capable and talented people allow their lives to be wasted. The plague of poverty curses millions who live in a world of abundance.

Bodies that should be vibrant and healthy in service to God and others, deteriorate by inactivity, disease and pain.

The gnawing, noxious cancers of negativism, resentment, remorse and despair poison the life-stream of thousands who could be a source of love and blessing.

These are the reasons for this book about God's big love-plan.

His love and mercy, His power and healing, His miracle presence in your life can bring an end to disease, defeat, poverty and despair.

He is good and He wills only good for you.

He is love and He yearns for you to share that love.

He is life and wants to pour that life into you.

He carries no whip and He wills no doom.

He created you in His image, so that makes you His kind of being.

HE PLANS ONLY GOOD FOR YOU

SHE LANGUISHED on a straw mat, on the earthen floor of her adobe hut, an emaciated, dying prostitute.

The cancer was terminal.

The Jesus-life transforms and recreates people.

What it means to be acquitted or exonerated.

No judgment for the believer who is restored to dignity and honor.

Chapter 12

She Looked Like An Angel

THE BIG LOVE-PLAN God offers to you involves an abundant and miracle lifestyle. Jesus said, *I am come that you might have life, and that you might have it more abundantly.*[Joh.10:10]

In one of our teaching crusades abroad, a prostitute who was dying of cancer was hauled to the meeting in an old wheelbarrow. Some Christians found her wasting away, languishing on a straw mat on the ground, in a tiny adobe hut where she had been abandoned to die.

When they told her about the crusade and offered to take her there, she was overwhelmed by their kindness. At first she objected because she was sure there was no hope for her ruined life. She had spent her years in prostitution and felt guilty and ashamed.

The Christians convinced her that *God had not sent his Son to the world to condemn the world; but that the world through him might be saved.*[Joh.3:17] They shared God's love-plan with her.

They placed pillows in the old wheelbarrow and hauled her to the meeting. Her emaciated body resembled a sallow skin-covered skeleton, except for her swollen cancer ridden abdomen.

Lying there in the wheelbarrow under the open sky, she listened to our teaching about the new life of Jesus Christ and how anyone can receive Him and His life into their heart by faith.

The Life-Giving Power of Love

I remember well my subject that night.

I spoke about receiving Christ and about the miracle that takes place when this new life is accepted by faith.

I emphasized God's love-plan and how Jesus died on the cross in our name, to suffer the judgment of our sins so that we could be restored to God as though we had never sinned. I stressed the fact that when we believe in His love-plan and accept what He accomplished for us, that we can receive Him into our lives and that when He comes to live in us, His life transforms us and creates in us a new person; that His life heals our sicknesses and regenerates us spiritually, mentally and physically.

When we finished the teaching and led the crowd of some 35,000 people in prayer to accept Christ, that woman repeated the prayer with us.

The realization of God's immeasurable love dawned upon her as she prayed to Him and received Him into her heart. She understood that since Christ bore all of the punishment for her sins, she was exonerated, acquitted, absolved from her sins and was no longer guilty.

She accepted her pardon and forgiveness and received Jesus Christ into her life by faith. His new life was imparted to her old nature and she was regenerated by the incomprehensible power of the life and love of Jesus Christ. She discovered the power of God's big love-plan.

Lying there, weeping for joy, overflowing with peace and thanksgiving, she looked up at her friends, reached out her bony arms to their strong hands and was raised up on her feet for the first time in months.

The Cancer Disappeared

As they wept and thanked God together, the dear woman suddenly realized that her tumor had disappeared and that her legs and arms had become strong.

She was not only forgiven of her sins and restored to dignity in God's family; she was also miraculously cured of the cancer.

She marched through the press of people, and up the steps of the platform. I can remember her standing there with tears streaming down her cheeks, with those bony arms raised toward heaven. Her upturned face looked like the face of an angel.

Her entire lifestyle was changed. *Old things were passed away; all things had become new.*[2Co.5:17]

She became a faithful and devoted follower of Christ and consecrated her life to helping other people to know about God's big love-plan.

What that woman received from God is the life and vigor, the happiness and health which Jesus Christ came to share with you and every one who believes in His love-plan.

Dr. T.L. and Dr. Daisy Osborn arrive in national attire at the big public field for another mass-evangelism crusade. They will share with more multitudes of needy people the message and ministry of God's non-judgmental, miracle LOVE-power.

In all of their teaching, preaching, writing and recording, they both emphasize the fact that *LOVE* is the *greatest power*, because "*God is love;*"[1Jo.4:8,16] that He values each person so highly that He laid down His life to redeem us from sin, guilt, disease and fear, lifting us out of despair and restoring us to God as members of His Royal Family and as His friends and partners in life.

The enduring focus of T.L. and Daisy's ministry to millions is to proclaim and demonstrate God's *LOVE* to humanity.

Damiano Bitatinya

SPECIAL SECTION
"MIRACLES OF LOVE"
PART I

DAMIANO'S MIRACLE

Damiano Bitatinya's miracle shook the city of Kampala and every one of the **multitude of people who witnessed it** take place. God impressed us to include this special miracle because the same compassion and love that touched and healed this poor, helpless man, can touch you too as you read about it.

This miracle account is a **modern up-to-date chapter in the continuing Book of Acts.** Read it with faith and expect to receive from God whatever you need, in Jesus' name!

I saw this poor man, clad in rags, near the Lugogo Stadium, staggering on trembling, incoherent legs, propped on two long poles, struggling alone toward our crusade grounds. Red dust was thick. The press of people was frantic. They were carrying lame and sick folks, leading the blind, etc. **But Damiano's lonely silhouette of despair would not leave my eyes.**

As I watched him from our car window, the Lord whispered to me: "God raises the poor out of the dust, and lifts the needy out of the dunghill; that he may set him with the princes of His people." Psa.113:7-8

I saw **the nation of Uganda,** in that forsaken, unloved, despairing man—alone, without hope or faith.

Daisy and I had come to this despairing, looted and brutalized nation, to tell them: **"Uganda, God loves you! God values you! God paid for you! He needs you! If you will believe on Him and reach out to Him, He will save and heal you and give you a new beginning!"**

As you read this, God is saying that to you, as much as He was saying it to those people in Uganda. His **touch of wonder** is reaching out to YOU—**now.**

We passed the poor man by as we rode into the grounds, but when I reached the platform, **I could not erase the silhouette of that lonely, hopeless and unloved human person from my mind.**

The Lord impressed me to call for him and to make an example of him before the multitude, to underscore the fact that God paid the same price for each person, and loved each one equally, regardless of how poor or sick or sinful anyone may be.

When I went to the microphone, I described the man to the people and they found him and helped him to come to me on the platform.

There before the multitude, I used him as an object lesson. I said, **"Even if you are poor, in rags, alone and sick, God values you. He has sent Daisy and me to tell you, HE NEEDS YOU! HE PAID FOR YOU! TRUST HIM, CALL ON HIM and HE WILL SAVE and HEAL YOU; He will GIVE YOU His NEW LIFE, and A NEW BEGINNING!"**

The people clapped and wept at the same time.

I called the poor man by his name: **"Damiano, you are special to God. You've begged and crawled long enough! I bring you good news! You are not forsaken. Jesus paid for you. He needs you! In His name I love you. Only believe!"**

I told the people: "What God does for this man, He will do for every Ugandan who believes!"

I told Damiano about Jesus and **he accepted Christ.**

I led him in prayer to be saved.

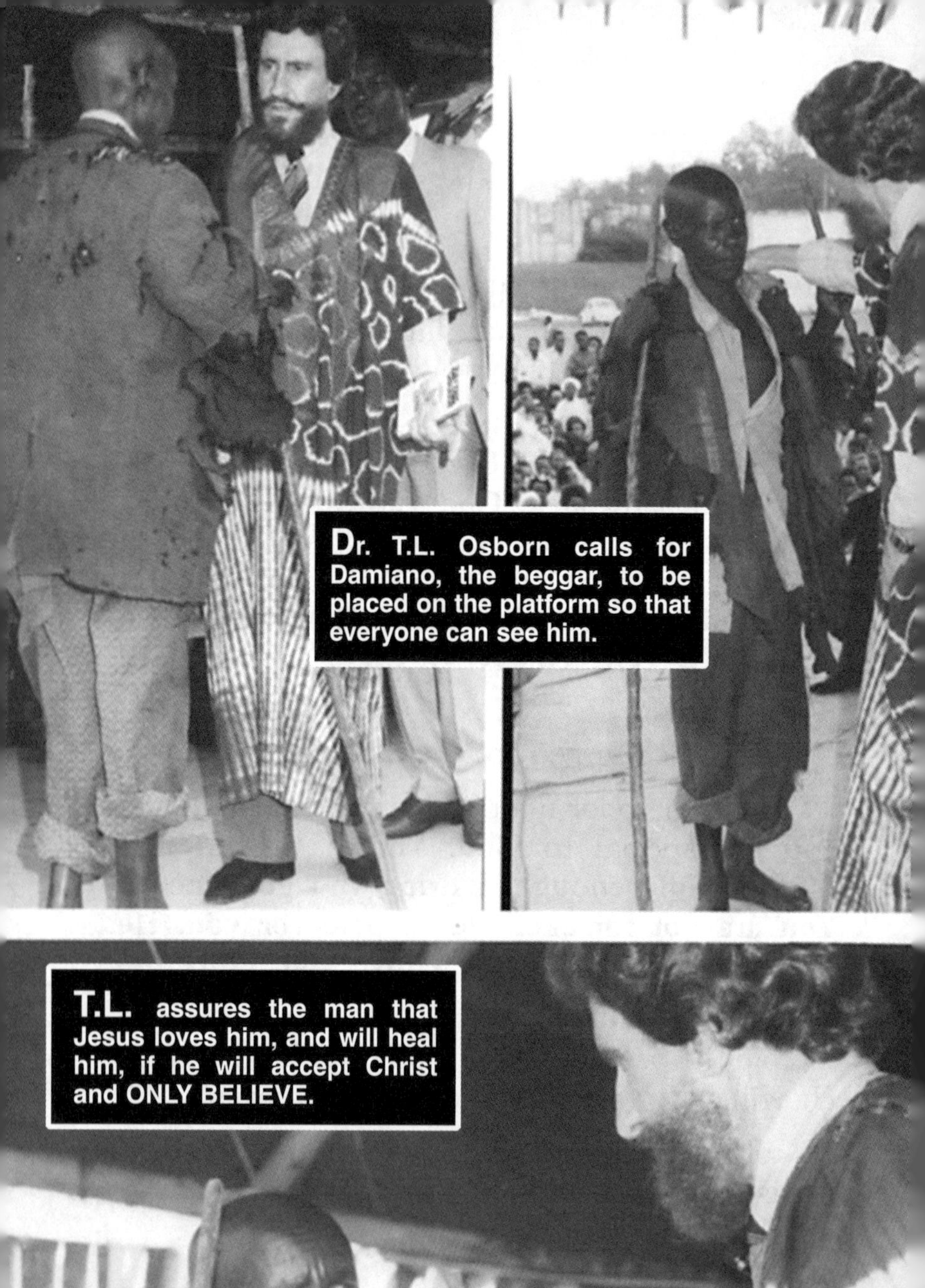

Dr. T.L. Osborn calls for Damiano, the beggar, to be placed on the platform so that everyone can see him.

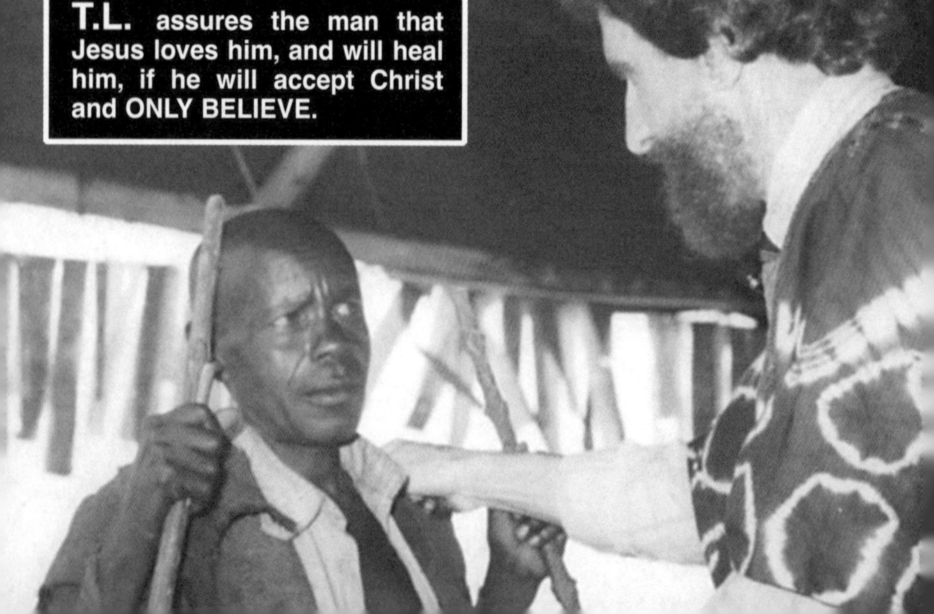

T.L. assures the man that Jesus loves him, and will heal him, if he will accept Christ and ONLY BELIEVE.

Then I pulled Damiano to me and I loved Him. I called out with a loud voice: **"Oh, you spirit of infirmity, leave this dear man forever, in Jesus' name!"**

Then I held him and imparted God's love and the healing presence of Jesus Christ.

I took the two poles from his hands and said, **"Damiano, you've staggered long enough. Animals crawl, but you are a man in God's image! Let's go! Walk! Jesus heals you! You are no longer a beggar! You are valuable! You are a child of God, with dignity and new life!"**

Damiano walked, taking strong steps! Then amidst tears, he broke into a glorious smile! The miracle was done!

He flung his arms around me in a grasp of love and gratitude. I'll never forget that embrace. **A beggar had become a prince in God's family!**

I said: **"Damiano, thank you for your love! Daisy and I are richer now because you are our new brother."** He was worth all that we did to bring God's love and miracle power to Uganda.

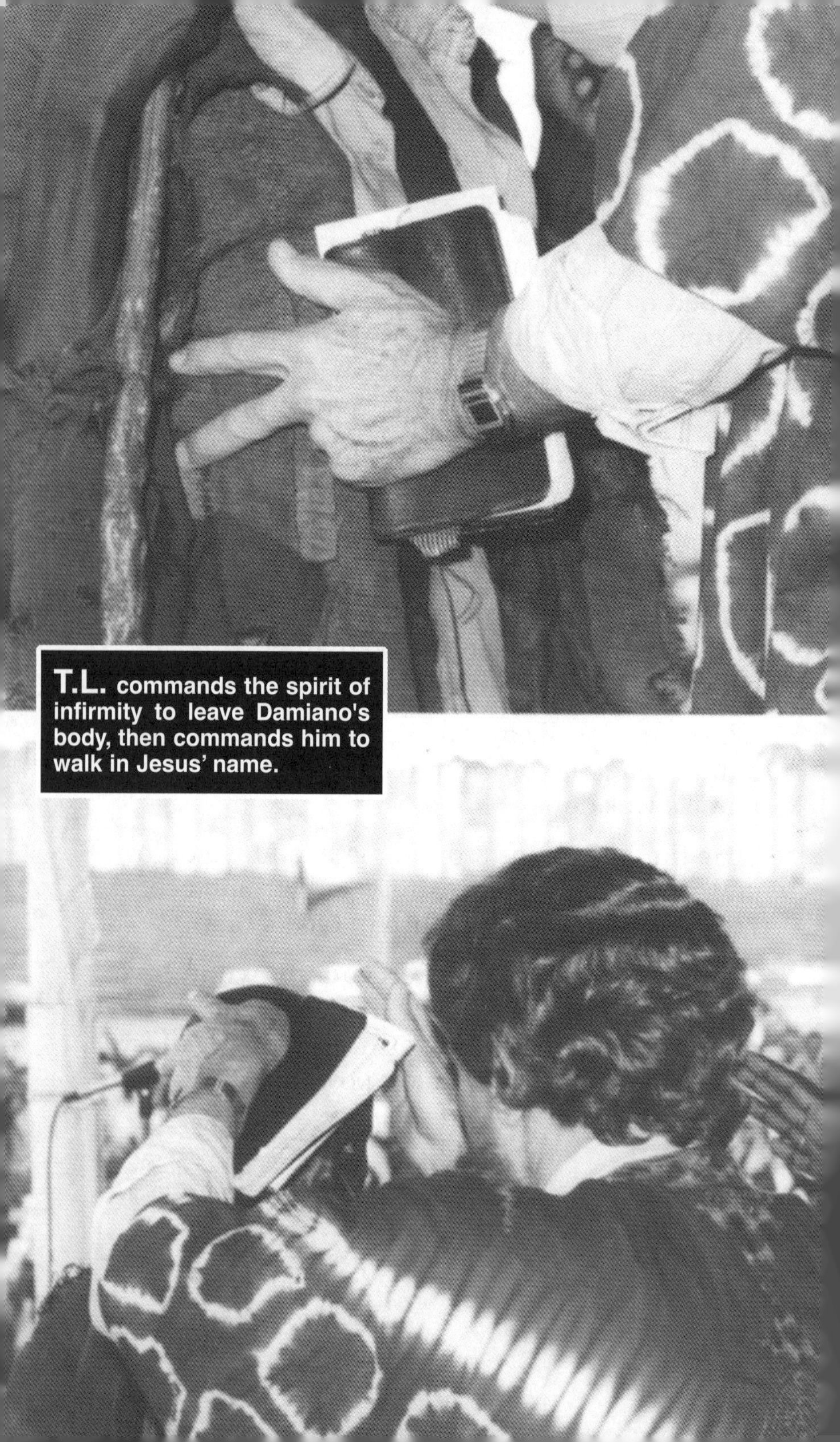

T.L. commands the spirit of infirmity to leave Damiano's body, then commands him to walk in Jesus' name.

Damiano walks with no support or help. He has been instantly healed.

To Daisy and me, **that is God's No. 1 Job!** To go to the forgotten, the lonely, the unloved, the disinherited, the sick, the fearful, those in despair...to go in Jesus' name and **to help them discover their value to God, and to humanity; to lift and heal and save them and to give them dignity, pride and salvation.**

I told Damiano: **"Sit in my chair. You are one of God's choice people now!"** As he sat there, smiling and happy, he looked like a PRINCE.

We arranged for Damiano to have good food, a bath, a bed and new clothes. The next day, he came **looking like a re-created wonder of God's love and power.** He embraced me and laid his head on my shoulder. **We were new friends!**

Damiano is one of thousands transformed in the Kampala Crusade. For over five decades, we have seen **Love's miracles** like this. In preachers and workers, it is another kind of miracle. Their message is changed from **condemnation** and **judgment** to **love** and **GOOD news.**

Damiano, our new brother, has been raised from despair to become a **member of royalty** through the compassion and powerful love of Jesus Christ.

Realizing that he is healed, Damiano embraces T.L. and thanks God for his miracle.

Damiano, clad in a new suit, returns to greet T.L. and Daisy and to witness of his miracle.

DAMIANO

By T.L. Osborn – October 3, 1985

A poem inspired by God,
recounting the miraculous healing of the beggar, Damiano,
during T.L. and Daisy Osborn's Mass Miracle Crusade
in Kampala, Uganda.

With no one to help, in the heat of the day,
I saw him alone in the throng;
Near the stadium gate, with sticks in his hands,
Damiano was staggering along.

I watched as we passed this friendless man
In despair, near the crusade grounds.
The multitude thronged, and dust filled the air;
In the mass, he could hardly be found.

But my eyes were fixed on his form—all along
And compassion rose up, deep inside.
We left him behind, but I could not forget
This beggar for whom Christ had died.

We were ushered onto the platform that day,
And an idea surged in my mind.
"Go get him, that ragged abandoned man!"
He's the picture of humankind.

At last, they brought him, confused and dismayed;
He stood there, enslaved and diseased;
His legs almost helpless, his eyes in a stare;
He asked: "What's happening to me?"

I told him how he was created by God;
How Christ died so he could be free;
How God's Love redeemed him so he could stand tall.
Amazed, he kept staring at me.

I told him that God never made him to crawl,
I embraced him and gave him God's Word.
I took his two sticks and cast them aside,
And I called on the name of the Lord.

God's Love overflowed as he reached out his arms.
Damiano became a new man.
He strode back and forth as the crowd clapped and wept;
He discovered himself in God's plan.

We loved him. We clothed him. I gave him my chair.
He sat like a prince by my side.
He is proof of the Gospel in action today.
He recovered self-value and pride.

We've witnessed innumerable wonders of Christ.
Damiano caused thousands to sing
Of God's Love and esteem; He had lifted him up
To new Life — and to walk like a king.

1985
GUEST

Dr. T.L. Osborn rescues beggar, Peter Musoke, from being overrun in the stadium exodus.

SPECIAL SECTION
"MIRACLES OF LOVE"
PART II

THE MIRACLE OF PAPA MUSOKE

Papa Musoke's miracle, during the Kampala, Uganda crusade, is **living proof of the great and beautiful wonders that God is doing through this ministry.**

Through this apostolic miracle, God is showing YOU that **Jesus is Unchanged** and that He will meet YOUR need today! Fresh, new faith for YOUR MIRACLE-NEED will be born in YOU, as you read about this wonder of God's love.

The great meeting that day had ended. Hundreds of miracles had been witnessed, and we were leaving the stadium. The vast multitude of people was bottlenecked, pushing to get out of the Lugogo Stadium grounds—and there I saw this **poor crippled beggar squeezed against the hedge, his paralyzed legs and feet about to be run over.**

Thousands of people were rushing to exit thru' the stadium gate.

BELOW: The beggar was pinned against the hedge, his crippled legs about to be overrun.

I jumped out of the car and halted the pressing river of people. As I looked at that lonely, frightened old man, the compassion of Jesus moved me to take a daring step of faith.

For years, Papa Musoke had been so lame and paralyzed in his back and legs, that he **could only move about by scooting along on his hips,** lifting and pushing himself with his hands. He had come to our crusade, but was not yet healed.

This poor beggar man was trying to scoot out of the gate in the press of people. **There he was, pinned against the bush at the wall, by a car whose wheels were about to over-run his feet.** I saw the dilemma just in time to jump out and STOP the crush of people—and the car.

I knelt in the dirt to help him and Jesus whispered to me: **"LOVE him! HEAL him and RAISE him up IN MY NAME!"** So I told him: **"Papa, Jesus loves you. God values you. He gave His Son for you. YOU are not made to crawl, but to walk like me! God paid as much for YOU as He paid for me. I will pray for you, then you can walk."**

Then I cried: "O you spirit of infirmity, come out of this dear man, in Jesus' name!" I KNEW it

T.L. tells Papa Musoke to "ONLY BELIEVE," then he prays for his healing.

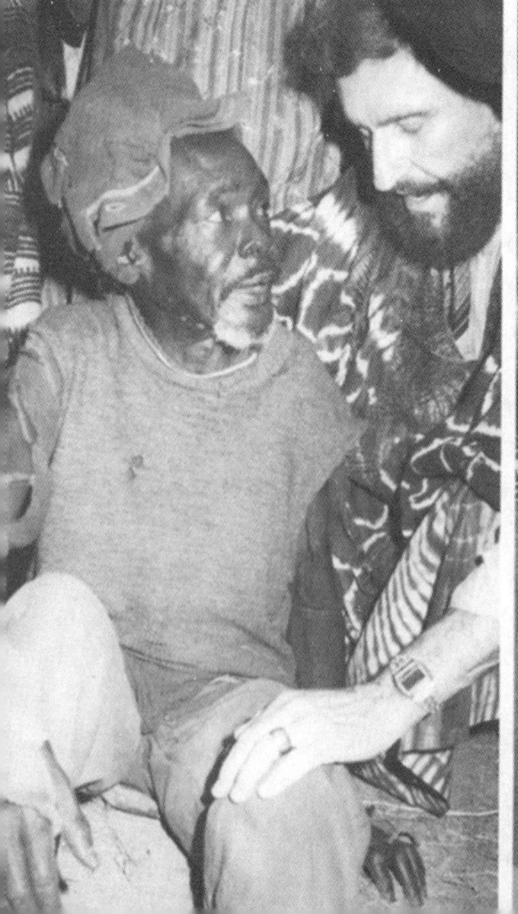

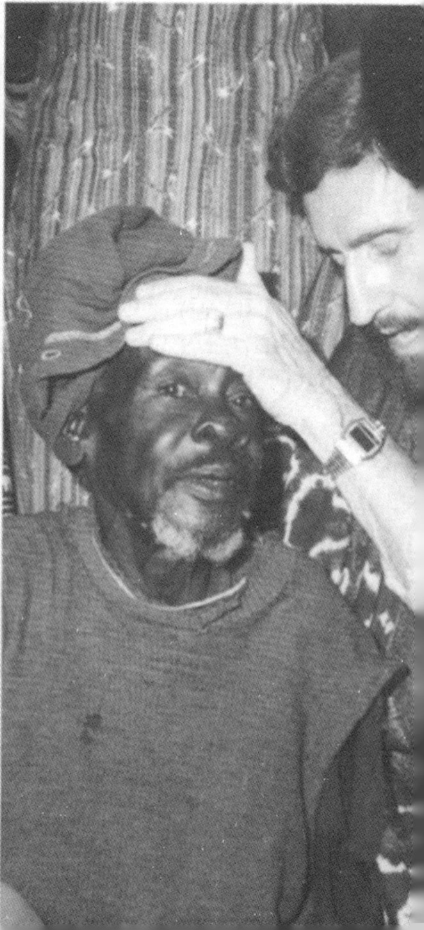

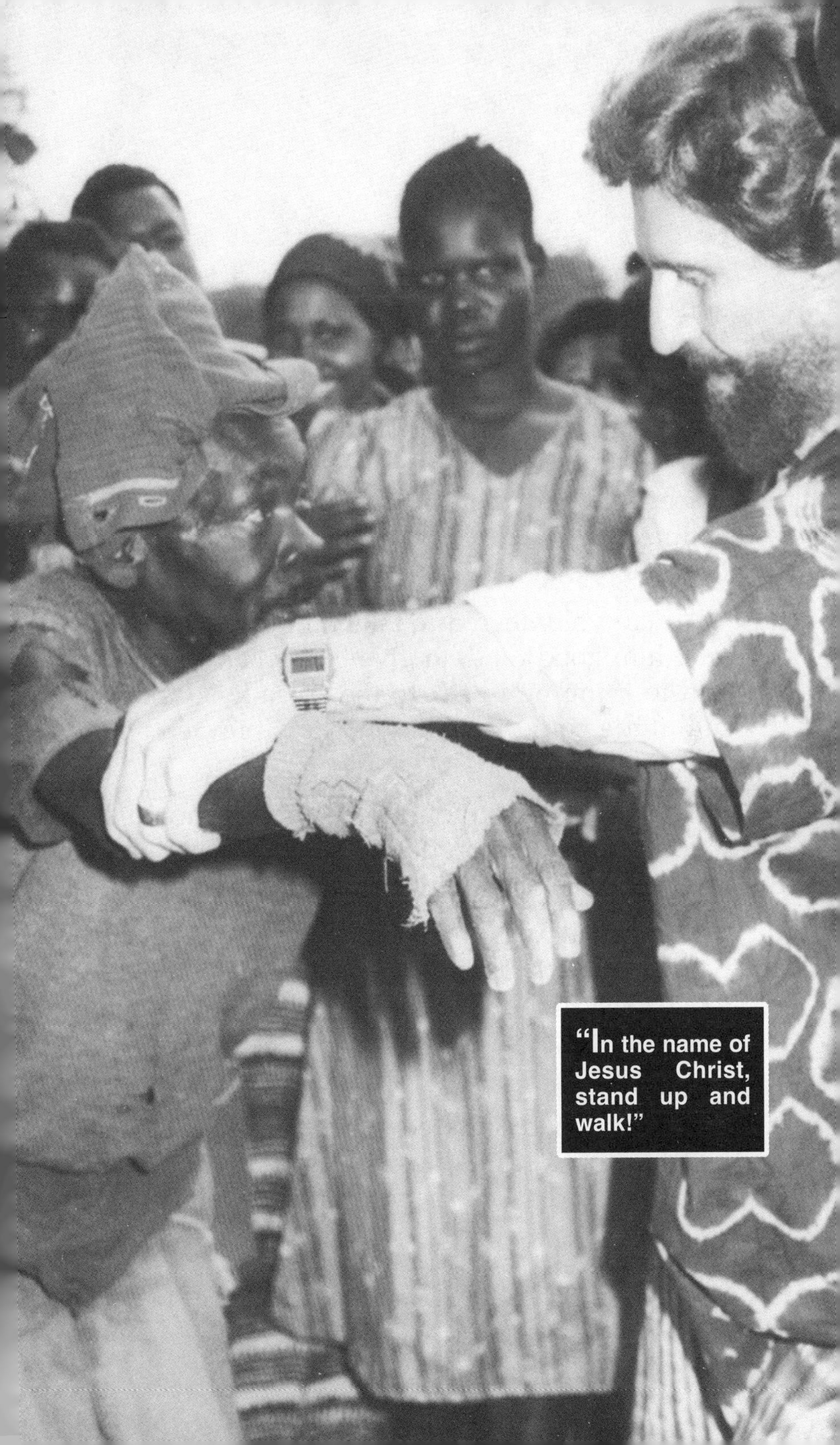
"In the name of Jesus Christ, stand up and walk!"

was done. I pulled him to me and I loved him, and Jesus' presence healed his bony emaciated body.

Then I took him by his arms and raised him up and HE WAS HEALED! The press of people went wild with joy as this BIBLE-DAY MIRACLE took place right out there in the middle of the road jammed with people. Hundreds believed on the Lord there that day.

A man volunteered to take him to his house, to feed him good food, to give him a bed to rest on, and to bring him back to the crusade so that the multitude could see him and hear him tell about his miracle.

No one had cared for him. He had no home. He had slept with some dogs that licked his hands and helped him to stay warm at night.

The next day as the mass of 200,000 to 400,000 people packed the grounds, I called for the beggar's new friend to bring Papa Musoke to the platform.

The dear old man explained how that for YEARS, he had suffered great pain and that he had to scoot on his hips to move about, and to beg for food. I asked the multitude to believe with

Papa Musoke realizes that Jesus has healed him.

Daisy and me for the COMPLETE MIRACLE, then we prayed again for him. As the healing virtue of Jesus Christ went into Musoke's body, hundreds more were healed too.

It was truly an apostolic miracle of mercy. Only God knows how many lives were changed in Uganda as that multitude **witnessed God's uncondemning, non-judgmental LOVE IN ACTION.**

I took Papa Musoke by the arm and walked with him, back and forth across the platform. As the crowd wept and applauded, the dear old man's face lit up in a smile as he realized **that this was not just a DREAM, but a REALITY.**

He was completely healed.

Then we arranged for a pastor to take charge of our new Christian brother. I told the pastor: **"Take him and give him good food, arrange for him to have a warm bath, give him a comfortable bed to sleep and to rest tonight. Then go buy him nice new clothes, shoes, a pretty necktie and whatever he needs to look nice. Bring him tomorrow for all to see!"**

The pastor did all he was told and brought to the platform, the following day, **a fine looking Christian gentleman whom no one recognized.**

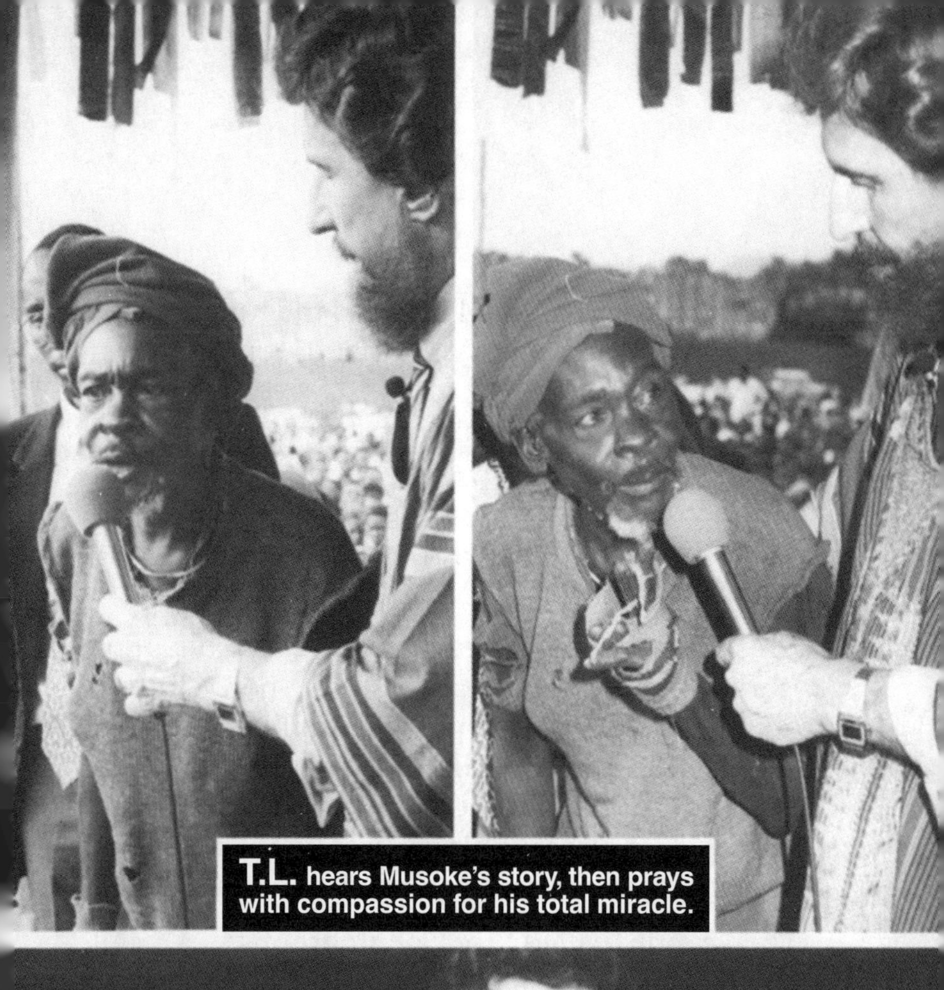

T.L. hears Musoke's story, then prays with compassion for his total miracle.

Then we called Papa Musoke to the microphone to tell the multitude what God had done for him, and when he stepped forward, everyone was shocked and broke out into spontaneous applause, rejoicing and even weeping. **They could not imagine the transformation of the ragged, despairing, crippled beggar they had seen the day before.**

Musoke was no longer scooting on his hips with his hands. He was dressed in new clothes, walking as well as anyone, and smiling with joy. **That was the GOSPEL IN ACTION—a hopeless beggar, lifted from the dust, from sleeping with the dogs, to a remarkably impressive gentleman, a redeemed, saved and healed man of God.**

The event called for photographs. We all wanted our pictures taken with Papa Musoke.

I wish the whole world could have seen **the pride and the delight which beamed in Musoke's face as he stepped by Dr. Daisy's side to be photographed with this remarkable lady of God.**

Daisy and I could hardly restrain our tears, as this wonder of God unfolded. There have been so many miracles for the deaf, blind, crippled, homeless, lonely and truly desperate people. It is impossible to describe the glory of the **beautiful and miraculous things we have witnessed here.**

The effect of such miracles is vital to the whole nation. Faith and hope are rekindled. Preachers are rising with new courage. The country is discovering that **the Jesus of the Bible is alive and unchanged today.**

Clad in the new clothes we got for him, Papa Musoke returns and we present him to the enormous crowd of people.

Papa Musoke gives thanks and shows the multitude how his life is now changed. Transformed by the love and power of Jesus Christ, he is now a child of God.

PAPA MUSOKE

By T.L. Osborn – January 12, 1986

A poem inspired by God,
recounting the miraculous healing of a beggar called Papa Musoke
during T.L. and Daisy Osborn's Mass Miracle Crusade
in Kampala, Uganda.

In the meeting that day, we had shown them The Way;
Then thousands pressed out through the gate.
The exit was jammed; the traffic was crammed,
We were trapped; I was almost too late.

T'was a poor beggar man, who walked with his hands;
His legs were helpless and dead.
He was hassled in haste by the mass at the gate;
His boney frame, so underfed.

He just crouched in the sand, this poor ragged man;
I could see from our automobile.
His legs near the brush, were about to be crushed
By the weight of advancing wheels.

I was stirred in my wrath and I jumped in the path
Of the car which had the man pinned.
I told them to HALT! That it wasn't his fault!
Then I knelt by this man — my new friend.

Frustrated and scared; bewildered, he stared.
Did I know he was there all along?
He was dirty and lost; he slept with the dogs,
Love was what he'd never known.

The exodus stopped. We were stifling hot
As hundreds engulfed us that day.

They were curious to see that poor beggar and me
On the ground. They just stared in dismay.

The man was alarmed as I reached out my arms
To rescue him out of the press.
Then I prayed to the Lord to give me His words
For this soul whom He wanted to bless.

An interpreter came and I talked of Christ's fame
To Musoke who'd known so much hurt.
I embraced him. I loved him. I told him that God
Never made him to scoot in the dirt.

"You've crawled long enough!" I said. Then I sighed,
With God's Spirit burning in me:
"He sent me to tell you that Jesus has died
To redeem you, so you can be free!"

We were truly besieged; we could hardly breathe.
I said, "Papa, your time is at hand!"
"God healed thousands today, and He wants me to say,
'It's for you too!' Get ready to stand!"

I charged the oppressing spirit to leave
That dear man, in Jesus Christ's Name.
I said, "On your feet! Stand and walk! You are free!"
He was healed! Proof that Christ is the same.

A man took him in, gave him food as a friend;
The next day he was dressed like a prince.
As the multitude gazed, the crowd was amazed,
And his fame has increased, ever since.

Through Papa Musoke, the Gospel is seen
As the power that saves from despair.
When we love folks and lift them, and give them esteem,
The world understands, that WE CARE!

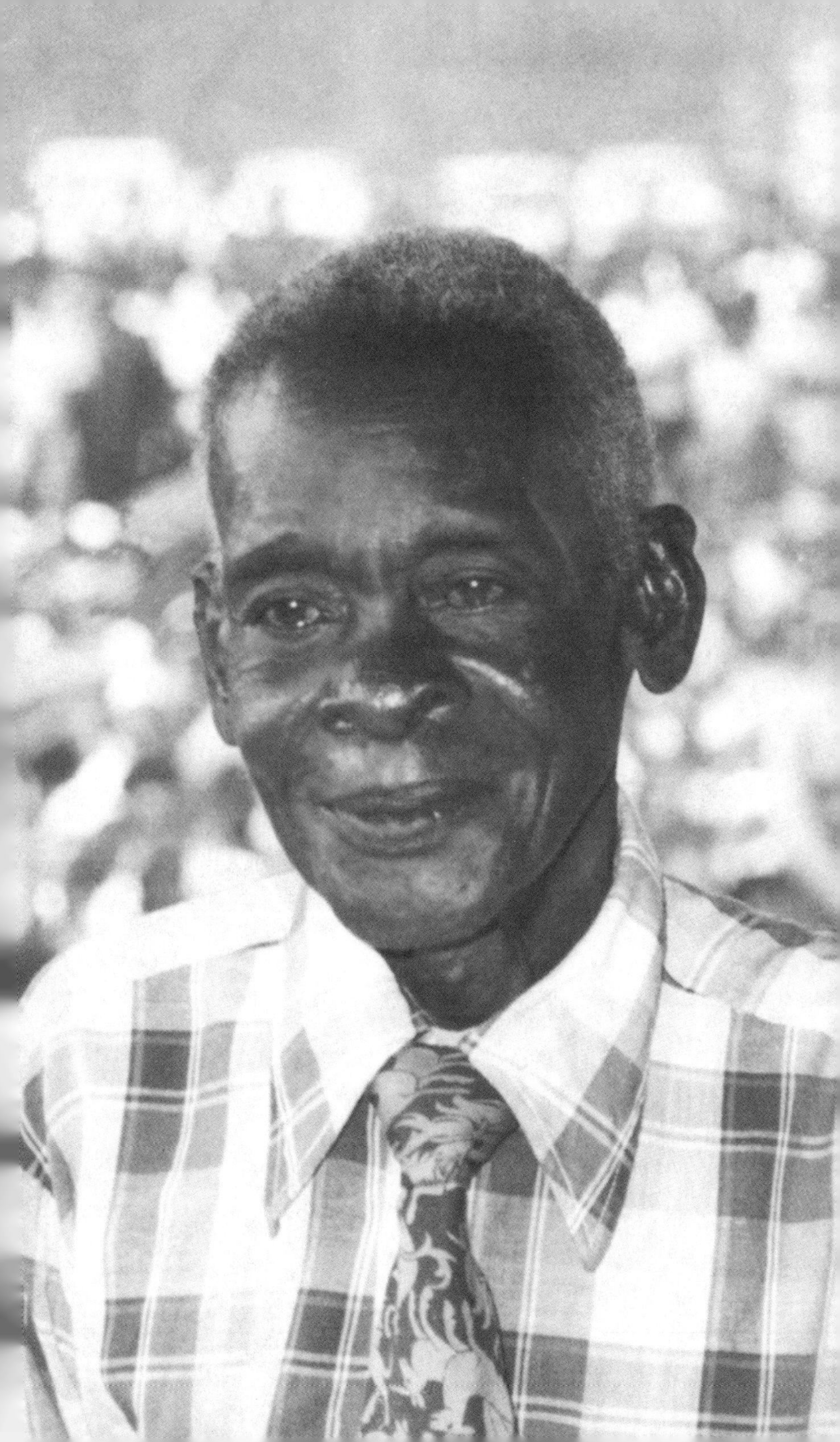

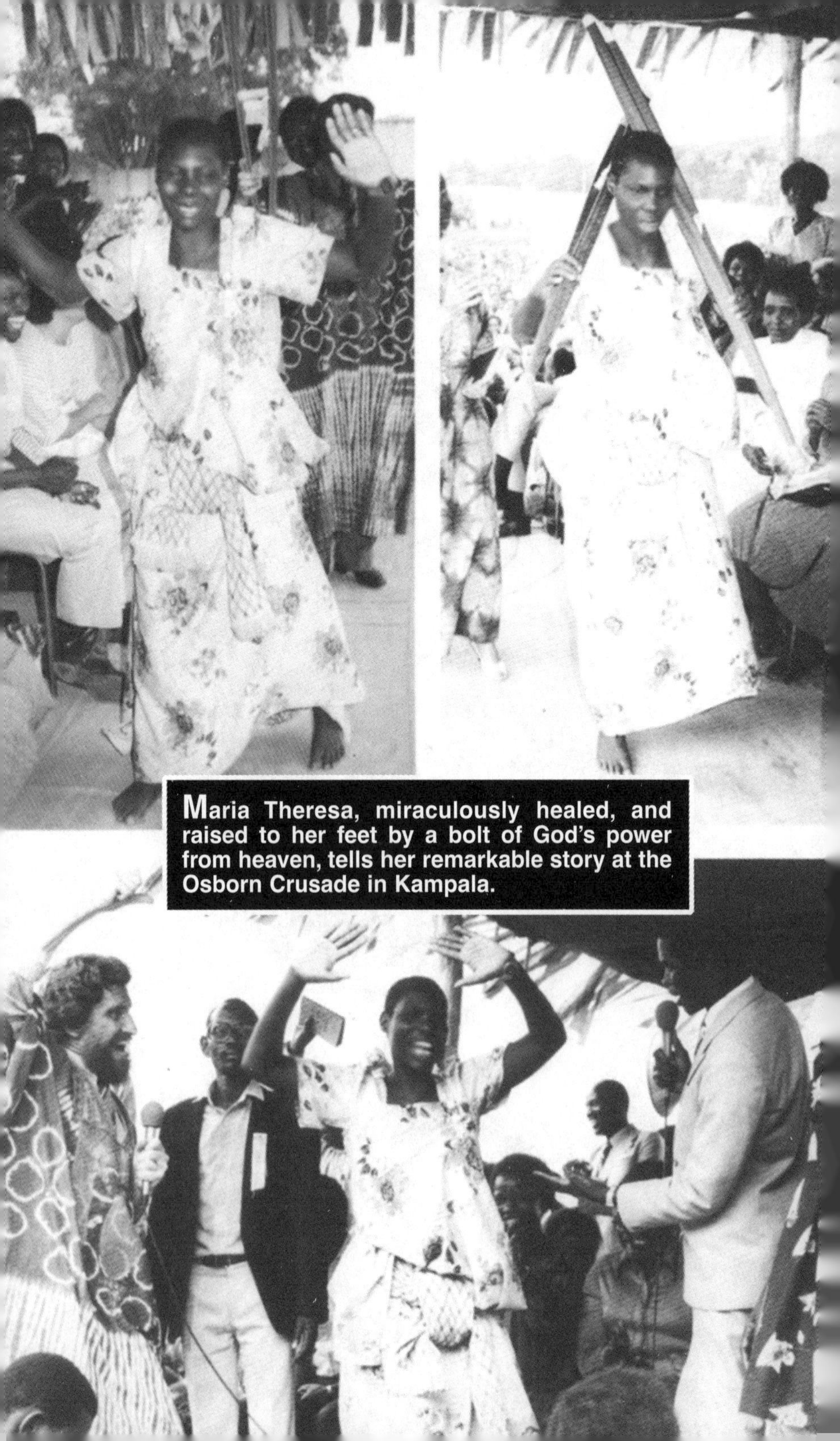

Maria Theresa, miraculously healed, and raised to her feet by a bolt of God's power from heaven, tells her remarkable story at the Osborn Crusade in Kampala.

SPECIAL SECTION
"MIRACLES OF LOVE"
PART III

MARIA THERESA'S MIRACULOUS HEALING

Maria Theresa had been sent home from the hospital to die. She had **no hope of ever walking again.** Several operations left here worse than before. She prayed to die.

Then news came of our crusade. **She was carried and laid on the ground amidst the throng.** Daisy preached about the woman bent double by a "spirit of infirmity."

Maria had rolled and agonized on the ground, in anguish and suffering. A painful bone disease deteriorated her spine and hips. (One had been dislocated for months.)

When Daisy spoke Christ's words, **"WOMAN, BE FREE!,"** Maria heard no more. She thought that it **thundered** and that **a bolt of lightning had struck her.** She was shocked to her feet, and healed, but was blinded by the power. She was stunned and she screamed for fear. People thought she was insane.

I went and caught her and brought her to Daisy, and when Daisy embraced her, **her sight was restored,** and she realized that she had been healed. She shouted, jumped and danced all over the platform and the mass of people was astounded.

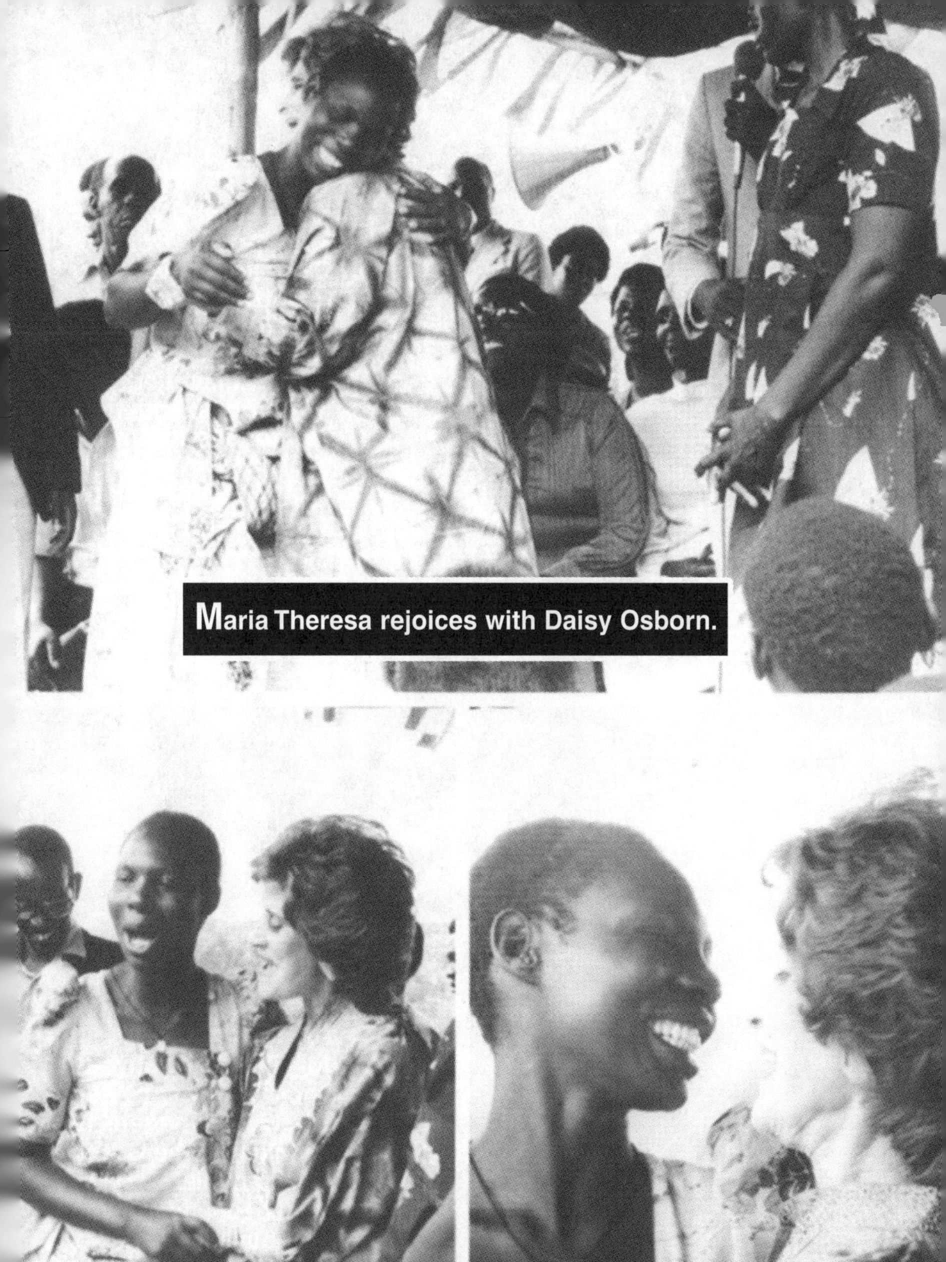

Maria Theresa rejoices with Daisy Osborn.

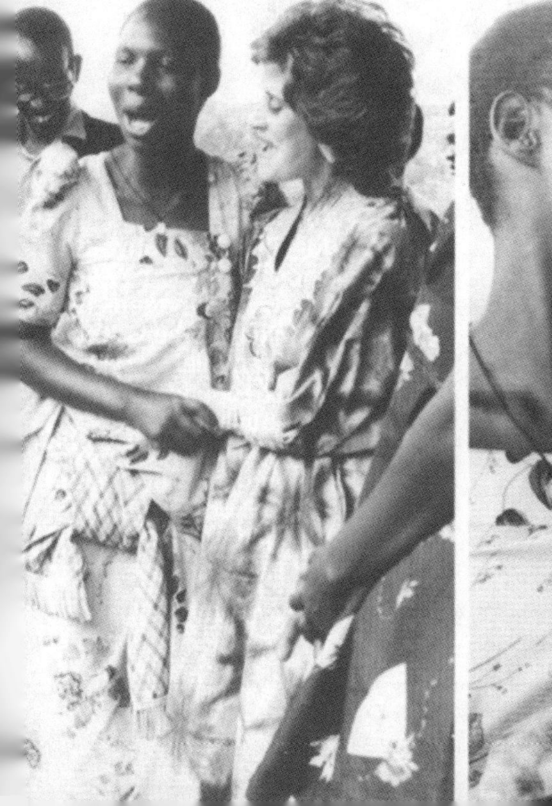

Betty Andiru was kidnapped from a Catholic convent by roving, rebel soldiers. They then took her to a secret jungle camp where they tied her with ropes and held her for months as a sex-slave, repeatedly raping her until she was driven insane.
For 13 years Betty was like an animal. She would bark like a dog and fight anyone who got near her. Friends managed to bring her to the Osborn Crusade. After Dr. Daisy preached and prayed for the mass of people, Betty was instantly restored, and she has since become an evangelist.

At the Lugogo Stadium in Kampala, Betty relates to Daisy, and to the public, the wonder of her miraculous healing. In a moving witness of God's love, she tells how Jesus brought forgiveness into her heart for those who brutalized her, and appeals to everyone to forgive whoever has wronged them during their civil war.

When Dr. T.L. saw Jesus alive in a vision in 1948, the ministries of T.L. & Daisy and their entire family – for generations to come – were forever changed. The healing power of Christ and His resurrection LIFE is the Osborns' central message.

Raised on the platforms of global miracle evangelism, Osborn daughter Dr. LaDonna's worldwide ministry is also marked by supernatural healing miracles. Why? Because Jesus and His ministry are the same TODAY as in Bible days.

Dr. LaDonna's lifetime involvement in mass miracle evangelism has equipped her to minister with ease and great authority, as shown here during the Osborn Festivals of Faith & Miracles in Kupang, Waingapu and Palangkaraya, Indonesia.

LaDonna Osborn Gospel Seminar & Book Distribution

LaDonna Osborn Festival of Faith & Miracles – Kupang, Indonesia

LaDonna Osborn Festival of Faith & Miracles – Waingapu, Indonesia

LaDonna Osborn Festival of Faith & Miracles – Palangkaraya, Indonesia

Waingapu, Indonesia

OSBORN MINISTRIES –

And he said unto them, Go ye into all the wc

OVER 60 YEARS – OVER 100 NATIONS

- Hong Kong
- India
- Indonesia
- Ireland
- Israel
- Italy
- Ivory Coast
- Jamaica
- Japan
- Kazakhstan
- Kenya
- Kyrgyzstan
- Laos
- Liberia
- Lithuania
- Luxemborg
- Madagascar
- Malawi
- Malaysia
- Mexico
- Mongolia
- Myanmar
- Netherlands
- New Zealand
- Nicaragua
- Nigeria
- Norway
- Pakistan
- Panama
- Papua N.Guinea
- Paraguay
- Peru
- Philippines
- Poland
- Portugal
- Puerto Rico
- Russia
- Rwanda
- Senegal
- South Africa
- South Korea
- Spain
- Sri Lanka
- Sweden
- Switzerland
- Taiwan
- Tajikistan
- Tanzania
- Thailand
- Togo
- Trinidad
- Uganda
- Ukraine
- United States
- Uruguay
- Uzbekistan
- Venezuela
- Vietnam
- Virgin Islands
- Zambia

preach the gospel to every creature. Mk. 16:15

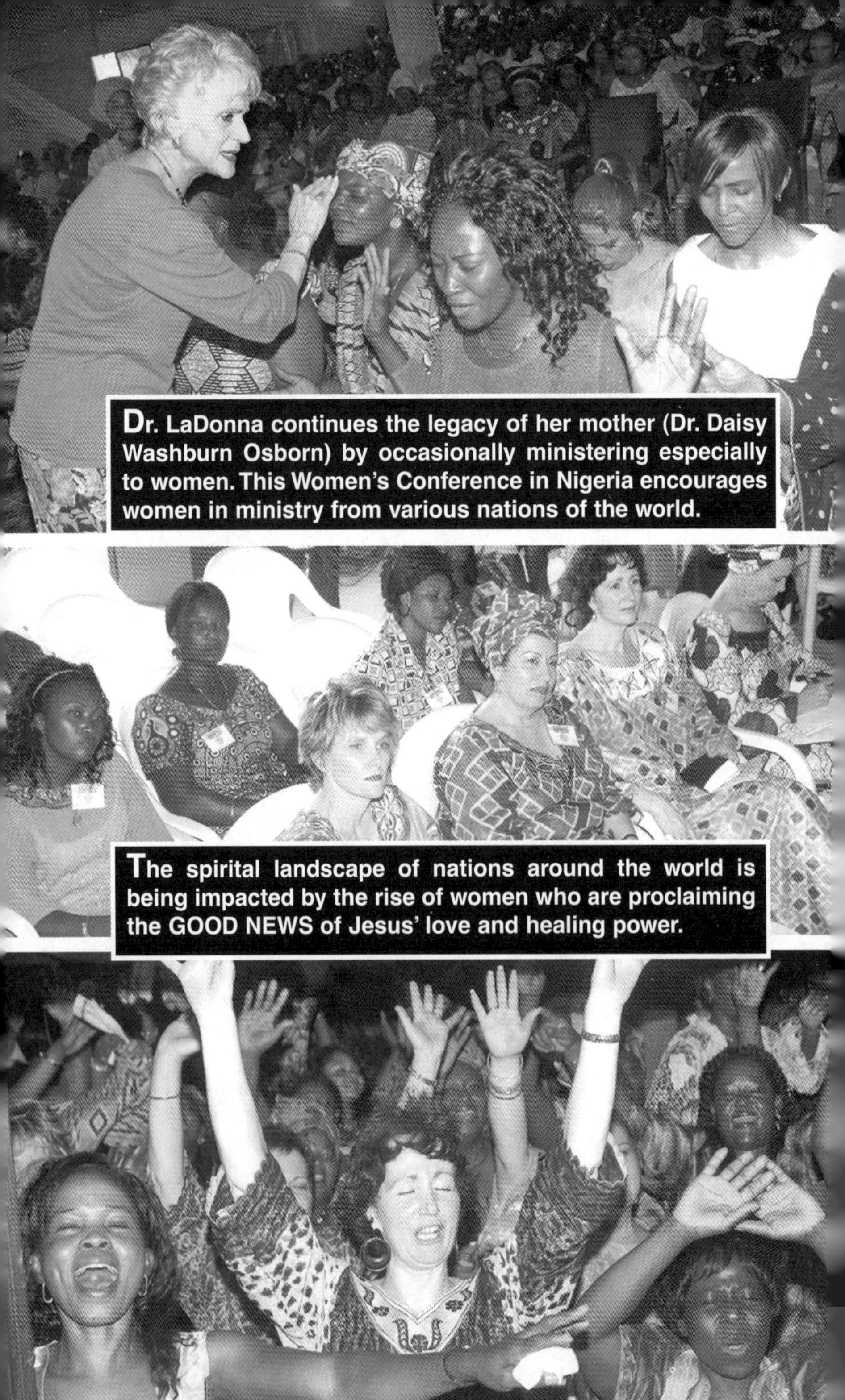

Dr. LaDonna continues the legacy of her mother (Dr. Daisy Washburn Osborn) by occasionally ministering especially to women. This Women's Conference in Nigeria encourages women in ministry from various nations of the world.

The spirital landscape of nations around the world is being impacted by the rise of women who are proclaiming the GOOD NEWS of Jesus' love and healing power.

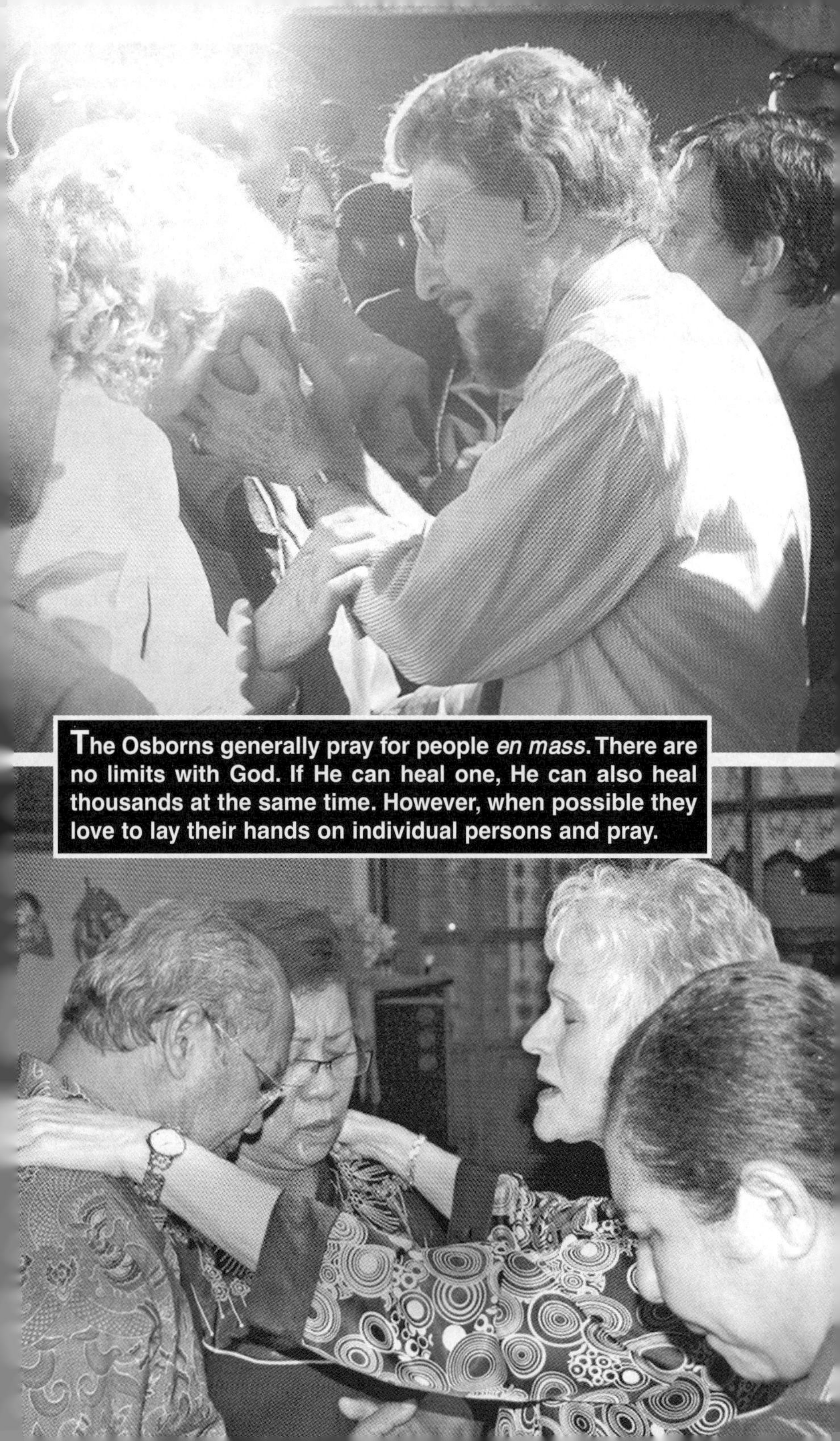

The Osborns generally pray for people *en mass.* There are no limits with God. If He can heal one, He can also heal thousands at the same time. However, when possible they love to lay their hands on individual persons and pray.

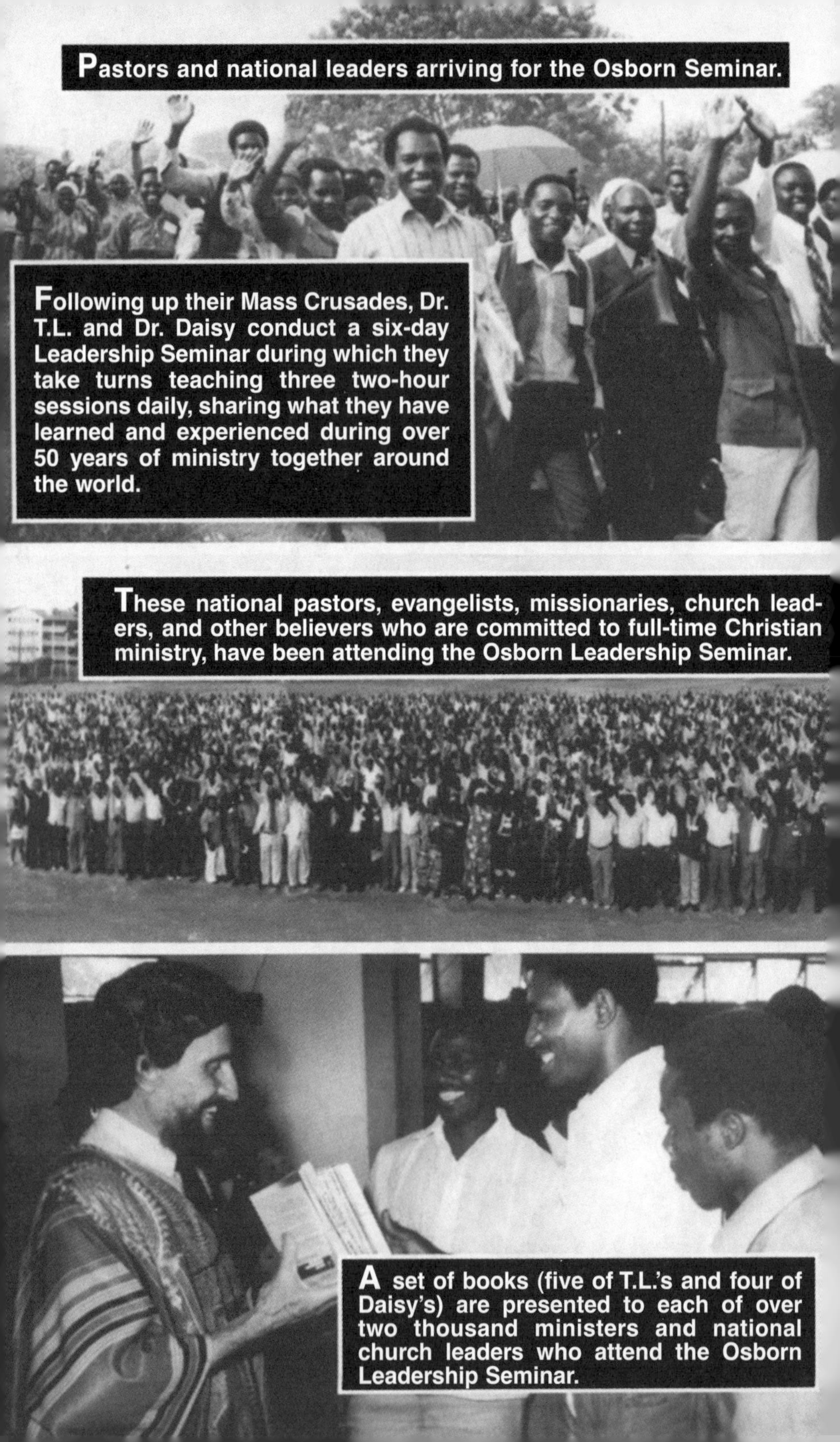

Pastors and national leaders arriving for the Osborn Seminar.

Following up their Mass Crusades, Dr. T.L. and Dr. Daisy conduct a six-day Leadership Seminar during which they take turns teaching three two-hour sessions daily, sharing what they have learned and experienced during over 50 years of ministry together around the world.

These national pastors, evangelists, missionaries, church leaders, and other believers who are committed to full-time Christian ministry, have been attending the Osborn Leadership Seminar.

A set of books (five of T.L.'s and four of Daisy's) are presented to each of over two thousand ministers and national church leaders who attend the Osborn Leadership Seminar.

The Osborn Leadership Seminar at Mombasa, Kenya where T.L. and Daisy share the secrets of success in gospel ministry with over 2,000 national preachers and ministers.

Now they assemble on an open ball field to pose for an official Seminar-photograph with the Osborns (front, center) who have shared six days of intensive teaching.

Dr. Daisy Osborn, with T.L., presents a set of nine of their dynamic books to each gospel minister who has attended the Leadership Seminar. She says: "Congratulations on your graduation! Here is good seed for good ministry. Sow it and reap a rich harvest of souls."

Tens of thousands of weary Congolese gather to hear a message of hope from Dr. LaDonna. Thousands believe on and accept Jesus Christ after hearing the Gospel, and marvelous miracles of healing are witnessed daily.

Dr. LaDonna Osborn is experiencing BIBLE DAYS in Point-Noire. "The blind receive their sight, and the lame walk ... the deaf hear ... and the poor have the Gospel preached to them."Mat11:5

– OSBORN EVANGELISM CRUSADES WORLDWIDE –

In over 100 different nations of the world, great multitudes always throng their meetings to hear God's word and to be blessed by Him.

Djakarta, Java, Indonesia
Yaba, Lagos, Nigeria, W. Africa
Hyderabad, Andhra Pradesh, India
Tainan, Taiwan
Guatemala City, Guatemala, Central America

The ministries of the Osborns have made an unprecedented impact on the world. They are considered by church leaders worldwide to be among the great soulwinners of our epoch. Dr. T.L. Osborn, Dr. Daisy Washburn Osborn (1924-1995) and Dr. LaDonna Osborn have ministered in over 100 nations.

THE PRICE GOD paid proves what He thinks of you, and proves the value of His word.

God's dream is beautiful.

How to relate God's love-plan to your problems, hurts and needs today.

The right to choose to trust the plan that works.

Five facts to trust.

Chapter 13

Your Way To The Good Life

GOD'S LOVE-PLAN for you, just like His original love-dream, is based on faith in His integrity, confidence and trust in His word. His only condition for you is that you simply honor and trust what He says, and He wants to honor and trust you.

At the cost of giving His own Son, God proved forever the integrity of His word.

The Bible says: *God promises, and does he not perform? Does he not carry out his word?* Num.23:19M

Here is what I mean.

God loved you and found a legal way to absolve you from every sin you ever committed.

Jesus came on a love mission to show you God's original dream for you. He lived a beautiful, inspiring life, without ever dishonoring God or questioning the integrity of His word.

Having lived without sin, He gave His life for you and died in your name, under the penalty of your sins, as your substitute. He bore all legal judgment that was against you.

Relate to God Through Christ and Live

How do you relate to what He did for you? How does it affect you in your problems and needs right now? What should you do about it?

The Bible says, *Whoever believes in Jesus Christ shall not perish* (or suffer the wages of sin which is death), *but have eternal life.*[Joh.3:16]

God's big love-plan is offered to anyone and to everyone who chooses to believe in His love. You are free to believe what He has said in the Bible and to accept His words as true.

Or you are free not to believe it. You have the personal right to carry on as you are, and to remain subject to disease, loneliness, inferiority and condemnation.

God's love-plan for you depends on your willingness to understand and believe that Jesus Christ died in your name, as your personal substitute, in your own place.

This is the key that unlocks God's blessings for you.

This involves **your** will.

You have the right of choice. You are free to accept the validity of what Christ did on your behalf, or to reject it as superstition or irrelevant or insignificant.

Trust the Plan That Works

God's big love-plan depends entirely on faith, just like He required Adam and Eve to trust His integrity.

The Bible makes some great statements about anyone who trusts in God's love.

Anyone who believes in Jesus Christ is not judged at all. Joh.3:18

All who trust God's Son to save them have eternal life. Joh.3:36

What specifically are you to trust or believe?

1. That Jesus was sinless and perfect;

2. That He died in your name, on your behalf and bore the judgment you should have borne;

3. That He did it because God loves you and wants to live with you;

4. That God values you so much that He paid this infinite price to make that possible;

5. That Jesus paid that price to restore you to God even before you knew you were estranged from Him. It was Love's idea to redeem you—not your idea.

Facts of Your Freedom

These remarkable facts are what constitute God's big love-plan.

Jesus Christ suffered the penalty of your sins so that you can be saved from death and live eternally as He planned for you.

He suffered the consequences of your sins so that you can be forever absolved from guilt, condemnation or judgment.

He took upon Himself your pains, infirmities and sicknesses, so that you can be free of them and live in health and enjoy longevity.

He bore your insecurity, shame, inferiority and loneliness, so that you can live in fellowship and friendship with God again.

He died so that you can live.

He assumed your guilt so that you can receive His righteousness.

God took the sinless Christ and poured into Him your sins. Then, in exchange, He pours God's goodness into you.[2Co.5:21LB]

The record of your sins was credited to Christ's account. Then He assumed your guilt and bore the judgment you deserved, in your name.

In exchange, His righteousness was credited to your account and you were declared righteous in God's eyes forever.

THE GREATEST idea of the big love-plan.

How to release dynamic love-power to reach out and to lift our world.

We cannot sustain hate. We can only live because we love. We are created by love. Love restores us to friendship and personal rapport with God.

The miracle of discovering self-worth, then discovering the value of people.

Chapter 14

God Values You And Needs You

THE GREATEST IDEA that God has ever shared with human persons is His big love-plan—the idea that we are valuable to Him and that He loves us so much that He has paid an incredible price for our happiness, health and success in life.

The love of God was proven toward us, because he sent his only begotten Son into the world that we might have life through him.[1Jo.4:9]

He wants us to live His kind of life—happy, productive, abundant, healthy.

The Bible says, *Herein is love, not that we loved God but that he loved us and sent his Son to be the sacrifice for our sins.*[1Jo.4:10]

God Can Now Live in You

You see, the miracle of the gospel is that we are restored to God by His love, not by anything we could ever do. As soon as we believe that, God can come back in us and live in us and through us like He originally planned, and carry out His work among people through us.

When Jesus, God's Son came and lived on this earth, He showed us the goodness, kindness and compassion of God at work among people. When God comes home to live in us like He lived in Christ, He wants to continue doing the same things He did through Jesus, because we are restored to Him, so now He can live in us.

Believing in God's big love-plan releases His dynamic love-power in us to reach out and help lift our world.

When God's love works in you and through you, that is God's power at work in you and through you. I call it God's love power.

When you reach out a hand to a fallen person and pick someone up, that is God's hand in action. The power of God's love is being extended through you. It is a miracle power, miracle love. There is no creative force in this world like the power of God's love at work in and through a human being.

We Can Live Because We Love

We must remember that God is love. Since we were created by God, we are the product of love. We are the offspring of love. It is natural for us to love. It is unnatural for us not to love.

Our nervous system cannot sustain hate. It will produce chemical poison in our system and cause disease to invade our physical body and to kill us prematurely.

Since Jesus Christ paid the full price for your sins, if you believe that He did it for you and in your name, that means you are legally free from all guilt, and nothing you have ever done can now separate you from God. You are restored to a position of friendship and rapport with Him. He is love. His emotions can now flow through you again.

The Love-Plan Took Root in Us

That is what happened to Daisy and me so many years ago when we welcomed Christ into our lives. As young people we were fortunate enough to hear about God's love-plan and we believed in it.

As a result, we felt that since Jesus had done such wonderful things for us, our lives would be given to tell others about Him and His love-plan.

When we were married at the young ages of seventeen and eighteen, we dedicated ourselves to sharing the gospel of Jesus with other people. When we were only twenty and twenty-one years old, we took our ten-month-old son and sailed to the other side of the world to share the gospel in India, to give the good news to the Moslems and to the Hindus of that land.

Now for over five decades, in nearly eighty different nations, we have travelled and taught God's big love-plan out in open stadiums or parks or fields, out where scores of thousands of people of all religions feel free to assemble without intimidation, and hear the teachings of Jesus Christ.

Perhaps we have taught the good news, face to face, to more millions of unchurched people than any other couple who ever lived. It is possible that we have seen more great healing miracles among the masses of unchurched people around the world, than any other couple on earth.

Discovering Self-Worth

God's love-power is working through us to reach people. We love them. We want to help them. God values them and needs them. We want them to know of His love and esteem for them. We know that if they discover God's love and esteem for them, they will begin to discover self-value and they will stop destroying and condemning and hating themselves and others.

We know that if people stop depreciating themselves, they will stop depreciating others. If they stop their self-destruction they will stop destroying others. If they can discover how much God values them, they will begin to value themselves and, in turn, they will begin to value others.

I think there is no life as great as to see people who are lonely, insecure, fearful, unloved, uncared for, forgotten or neglected, and to be able to give them the message of God's big love-plan that helps them stand up and straighten their shoulders, to lift their heads and to walk with a long stride, realizing that they count with God.

To lift people and to help them discover the rich and purposeful life God created them for, to help them discover that God loves them, that Jesus gave His life for them; *to lift beggars out of the dunghill and to set them on high with God,*[1Sa.2:8; Psa.113:7-8] as the Bible says, that is the greatest life on earth. That is the power of God's big love-plan in action.

You see, that is what God has done for us, and that is what He now does through us as we share His love-plan with others.

That is the reason this book is in your hands. God is saying to you:

> **"I love you. I value you. The price I paid for you proves what I think you are worth.**
>
> **"Believe in my love-plan and let me restore to you the riches, the happiness, the health and the abundance I created for you.**
>
> **"Then I will be able to reach out to others through you, and in that way, your life will fulfill its divine purpose as you discover the happiness of becoming my friend and partner in helping others."**

A NEW understanding of God's love. People in nearly 80 nations discover the same power and react the same way.

Alaskan Eskimos, American Indians, Japanese Shintoists, Thai Buddhists, Javanese Moslems, Indian Hindus, African Animists, Western Christians, share the same search.

The Buddhist nun discovered peace after her 74 year quest.

Chapter 15

The Buddhist Found The Way

I CAN ASSURE you that the contents of this book work. As you read it through, with your heart open and sincere, I am sure that you are experiencing a new understanding of God's love.

We have watched thousands of Moslems, Buddhists, Shintoists, Hindus, fetish-worshippers, atheists and nominal Christians turn to Jesus Christ and receive Him into their hearts and become radiant new creatures as soon as they came to understand the simple but powerful facts of God's big love-plan you are now discovering.

No Difference in People

I can tell you that people are basically the same worldwide. They commit the same sins, experience the same needs, sense the same guilt, suffer the same diseases and instinctively search for the same peace, regardless of race, sex, color, nationality or background.

When people really understand God's big love-plan, they react with the same overwhelming satisfaction. I have watched thousands of stoic and traditionally calm American Indians, Eskimos and Japanese people experience the wonder of God's new life. The effect upon their lives is no different than what happened to people in Bible days.

We have watched hundreds of mature Moslems experience this miracle in a single night and react the same as one might expect to see in the West.

We have observed placid and poised Buddhists break into tears of gratitude as they believed on Jesus Christ and discovered His love for them.

We have proven what the Bible says: *For there is no difference...the same Lord over all is rich unto all who call on him, for whoever shall call on the name of the Lord shall be saved.* Rom.10:12-13

At 74, She Heard the Love-Plan

During our crusade in southern Thailand, a 74-year-old Buddhist nun attended. She was placed in the temple when she was only a girl and had consecrated her life to serve the temple.

Our teaching meetings were conducted out under the shade of a huge coconut palm grove. The sound from our loud speaker horns reached her ears.

She slipped away from the temple and bought a piece of cloth in the market place with which she could conceal her identity, since her only clothing was a nun's habit.

She stood in a shadowy area at the edge of the field to avoid recognition.

That night I spoke about God's big love-plan and how the good news of what Jesus did on the cross is for us. I quoted various scriptures which explained how humanity had sinned, how God loved us and valued us so much that He gave His Son for us, how Jesus bore the sin and guilt and condemnation that we deserved and how He died in our place, was buried and then rose from the dead, and that He lives today and wants to come into our lives in order to share God's abundant life, His peace, forgiveness, health and blessing with us.

That old woman had never heard those gospel facts in all of her life.

The Beautiful Report

She came to our cottage the next day. We sat for two hours out under those beautiful palm trees as she tried to tell us, through the interpreter, what had happened.

Her eyes glistened like a young maiden's, as she explained how she had received Jesus Christ and had been made new inside.

She said, "All of my life, I searched for peace. The only thing I knew to do was to work hard in the temple and to serve the priests every way possible.

"I soon learned that everyone in the temple was searching for the same peace that I sought, but that we were all unsatisfied. The others were as unhappy as I was.

"I often wondered if there was anything else I could do to find peace in my heart. Many nights, I wept for hours in the darkness when no one could see me. I felt guilt but I knew no way to find peace.

"The first time I listened to you, Dr. Osborn, when you talked about God loving me and sending His Son to die on the cross for me, and how His blood was shed for the remission of my sins, I felt something happening inside of me. At last someone had come and was showing me the way to find peace. I wept and wept. I believed what you said about Jesus. I didn't fully understand it but I believed it and I felt that my whole life was being transformed by a miracle.

"I repeated your prayer as you directed us. Oh what peace came into my heart when I welcomed Jesus into my life. I felt no guilt or shame before God. I felt I had recovered dignity. I was identified with Jesus. I knew I was saved. I had a new life.

"Now the rest of my life shall be consecrated to telling others about Jesus Christ, God's Son who is my savior. I am so happy."

That dear old woman went back to the village of her people to tell them about Jesus. It was not long before she was teaching groups of them about God's big love-plan and together, they built a bamboo and thatch meeting house which soon became a thriving church in that village.

You can experience the discovery of peace and dignity with God, while you are reading this book.

WHEN OUR foreparents rejected the integrity of God's word, the human race was disqualified to live on God's level.

Seven needs resulted.

Seven provisions of the big love-plan.

Seven wonders of the new lifestyle.

Seven names that identify us with greatness, happiness, health and abundance.

Chapter 16

Seven Needs Supplied

GOD CREATED US perfect in the beginning. Then Adam and Eve betrayed God's trust and doubted the integrity of His word. The result was the general deterioration of humankind: sin, sickness, weakness, failure, loneliness, fear, hatred, murder, revenge, jealousy, confusion, guilt, emptiness, condemnation and death—eternal separation from God.

When our foreparents, Adam and Eve, rejected the integrity of God's word, and believed what Satan said, the human race was thereby disqualified to live on God's level, and therefore became subservient to Satan whose design was to deceive and to destroy God's wonderful human creations.

But God did not want us to live in shame, to be condemned, to die.

Through the death of Christ on the cross for us, He paid the full price for our restoration.

Our needs are sevenfold.

God's nature is sevenfold.

Christ's provision is sevenfold

Redemption is sevenfold.

What do I mean by redemption?

The dictionary defines it: To buy back, to repurchase, to free from captivity, to release from debt or obligation or blame.

Seven Revelations of God

God reveals Himself by seven redemptive names, showing His sevenfold nature which imparts His sevenfold blessings to our lives. Everything we can need or desire is provided for us through Christ.

God's big love-plan incorporates redemption for all of the aspects of our nature. He created us in His image; we are like Him. His nature has seven aspects. So He has shown each aspect of His love-nature by giving us a redemptive name by which to call Him.

According to the world-renowned Scofield Bible, page 7, item (4) under the commentary on Genesis 2:4, the seven redemptive names of God are outlined as follows:

God is our RIGHTEOUSNESS (Jehovah-tsidkenu).[Jer.23:6; Rom.3:24-25; Phi.3:9]

God is our PEACE (Jehovah-shalom).[Jdg.6:24; Eph. 2:14; Col.1:20]

God is our GUIDE or SHEPHERD (Jehovah-ra'ah).[Psa.23:1; Joh.10:7,11]

God is our PHYSICIAN or HEALER (Jehovah-rapha).[Exo.15:26; Mat.8:16-17]

God is our PROVIDER or SOURCE (Jehovah-jireh).[Gen.22:13-14; Phi.4:19]

God is EVER PRESENT (Jehovah-shammah).[Eze.48:35; Exo.33:14-15; Mat.28:20; Heb.13:5]

God is our VICTORY (Jehovah-nissi).[Exo.17:14-15; Col.2:14-15; 1Co.15:57; Rom.8:37-39]

There Are No Exceptions

This may sound terribly theological, but the next chapter will show you the practical ways this all applies to you.

These seven names reveal the seven aspects of God's nature represented in the seven redemptive blessings which He restored to every person on earth who believes in His love-plan.

There are no exceptions in Christ's redemptive work. Every blessing provided by the death of Christ on the cross belongs to every person in the world for whom He died—that is EVERYONE. They are for "whoever," a word used over 100 times in the New Testament alone.

DIVINE Dignity
Perpetual Peace
Dependable Direction
Hearty Health
Productive Prosperity
Constant Companionship
Accomplished Achievement

Chapter 17

Seven Blessings Are Yours

I WANT TO enumerate for you the seven fundamental blessings which the death of Christ has already paid for. All of them are for YOU from the moment you believe in God's big love-plan.

I. DIVINE DIGNITY

The Lord Our Righteousness

We are no longer condemned by our own resentment, jealousy and guilt. God's love-plan transfers to our account the righteousness and dignity of the greatest life ever lived, that of Jesus Christ, and His new life becomes ours.

We are no longer under the sentence of death because of our sins.[Rom.6:23; Eze.18:20]

The Lord is our righteousness. God has credited the righteousness of His Son to our account. We can now have His life and His nature,[2Co.5:21] if we believe that Jesus died on the cross to pay the penalty for our personal sins.[1Pe.2:24]

II. PERPETUAL PEACE

The Lord Our Peace

We are no longer living in torment with ourselves, out of harmony with family and friends. We are no longer transferring these mental anguishes to our own bodies, to our businesses, to our environment. We are no longer ruining our own health and happiness by their poison. God's love-plan changes us and transfers His peace, tranquility and harmony to us and makes us new persons.

We are no longer guilty or tormented by our sins and transgressions.[Isa.1:18; Col.1:13-14] We no longer fear God and dread judgment.[2Co.5:10; Rom. 5:18; 1Jo.4:17] Jesus Christ assumed all judgment for our sins and there is nothing now against us when we believe in God's big love-plan.

The Lord is our peace. He bore our judgment and suffered the punishment for all of our sins.[Isa.53:4-5,8,10-12] Since no penalty can be paid twice, we can be free and saved. We can have peace. We can be well, as soon as we *only believe*[Mar.5:36] in His love-plan.

III. DEPENDABLE DIRECTION

The Lord Our Shepherd

We are no longer going on in confusion, making wrong decisions, stumbling into failure and every conceivable trap of defeat. God's love-plan gives us direction and guidance in life so that we will enjoy success, health, prosperity and fulfillment.

We are no longer deceived and perplexed, confused and misguided.

The Lord is our shepherd,[Psa.23:1; Joh.10:14] our unfailing guide, our director. He takes control of our lives. When we follow Him we are on the right road.[Joh.8:12;14:6] The good shepherd gave His life for the sheep, to show us the way.[Joh.10:11;15:13] Now we look to Him and hear His voice and follow Him in the way [Joh.10:27-28] of true life and health, success and abundance.

IV. HEARTY HEALTH

The Lord Our Physician

We are no longer subjecting ourselves to disease and sickness, living vulnerable to every physical plague that ravages human beings. God's love-plan includes His abundant miracle power to heal us not only of diseases, allergies and infirmities, but also to keep us in health, physically fit and with long life.

The Lord is our physician.[Isa.53:4-5; Mat.8:17] In His death on the cross, He bore our sicknesses, suffered our pains and carried our infirmities. Since they were ours, and He did it in our place, *by his sufferings, we are healed.*[Exo.15:26; 1Pe.2:24]

You can receive a healing miracle while you read this book.

V. PRODUCTIVE PROSPERITY

The Lord Our Provider

We are no longer believing in poverty and want. We are no longer victims of circumstances. We are no longer living our lives on a hand-to-mouth basis. God's love-plan includes all of the wealth of this world. He created it and placed it here for our blessing and prosperity. So we take Him into personal partnership for life.

We are no longer the slaves of poverty, lack or material privation.

Christ put aside all of His riches and became poor for us, so that He might redeem us from want and impart to us His riches.[2Co.8:9] Now we share His unlimited supply.[Joh.10:10] We enjoy His plenty.

The Lord is our provider. Through His love-plan, He enters our lives and shares with us his abundant living.

VI. CONSTANT COMPANIONSHIP

The Lord Our Present Friend

We are no longer lonely and fearful, discouraged and depressed. God's love-plan includes His guarantee to become our companion. He actually lives in us and with us as our personal friend. We now know only the success, happiness, health and prosperity that is assured when God is our partner.

We are no longer walking life's road alone. We are no longer forsaken and lonely, unvalued and unloved.[Isa.41:10]

The Lord is our present friend. His love-plan guarantees His presence with us. The Lord pledges Himself to be with us always, by our side, in us.[Pro.18:24; Col.1:27; 2Co.6:16] He died to put away our sins so that He could be our personal friend and walk with us again,[1Jo.1:3] hand in hand, throughout this life and throughout eternity.

VII. ACCOMPLISHED ACHIEVEMENT

The Lord Our Victory

We are no longer trying and failing in life. We are no longer lacking accomplishment and devoid of success. God's love-plan makes us a constant winner because He is on our team. We discover the good life with the guarantee of God's abundance and success. We shall never spend our days drinking the dregs of leftovers. Success, accomplishment and achievement are built into our very natures and we are God-created human persons with dignity and with honor.

We are no longer enslaved by defeat or failure. We are no longer held captive by evil or dominated by the works of Satan.[Col.1:13; 1Jo.5:18]

The Lord is our victory. He died *to destroy the works of the devil.*[1Jo.3:8] He arose from the dead with the proclamation: *All power is given unto Me in heaven and earth...and, lo, I am with you alway.*[Mat. 28:18,20]

SEVEN BLESSINGS ARE YOURS

THE MIRACLE moment that triggers a new lifestyle.

There was no way of escape, but love had a great idea.

When God can come home in you and you can come home in God.

There is no more failure, loneliness, insecurity, disease or inferiority.

Chapter 18

Miracles Of The Love-Plan

WHEN DO THE seven blessings which Christ paid for become yours? When can you realize them in your own life?

From the moment you decide to relate with what Jesus Christ did in His death for you on the cross. From the moment you believe that He assumed the judgment for your sins, in your name and in your place. When you do that, you will begin to experience the miracle of His love-plan at work in you.

These are some of the things that will take place in your life and on your behalf.

1. The righteousness of Christ will be transferred to you and you will be free of all guilt and judgment.

2. Jesus Christ will come and live the life of God in and through you.

3. You will become a new creation.

4. You will be restored to God with dignity and honor, according to His original love-plan.

5. A supernatural power will be given to you which will make you a child of God. It will be a miracle.

Christ opened the way for God to come to you and for you to come to him. He is your link with God, your way to the good life.

Treasures of Faith

Here are several Bible verses that you will now understand and will want to remember as treasures of faith. (I have personalized them for you.)

Now, since you have been made right in God's sight by faith in his promise, you can have real peace with him because of what Jesus has done for you. Rom.5:1LB

When you were utterly with no way of escape, Christ came…and died for you when you had no use for him. Rom.5:6LB

God showed his great love for you by sending Christ to die for you while you were still a sinner. Rom.5:8LB

Now God has declared you not guilty. Now he will save you from all wrath to come. Rom.5:9LB

Now you can rejoice in your wonderful new relationship with God – all because of what your Lord Jesus Christ has done in dying for your sins – making you a friend of God. Rom.5:11LB

God says, I will dwell in you, and walk in you, and I will be your God and you shall be my child.[2Co.6:16]

God promises, I will never leave you or forsake you. [Heb.13:5]

I will be a Father unto you, and you shall be my child, says the Lord Almighty.[2Co.6:18]

And…whoever shall call on the name of the Lord shall be saved.[Acs.2:21]

For there is salvation in none other: for there is no other name under heaven given among people by which you can be saved.[Acs.4:12]

My prayer for you is that you may be as healthy and prosperous in every way as you are in your soul. [3Jo.2PME]

There is no condemnation (judgment, penalty) *awaiting those who belong to Christ Jesus.*[Rom.8:1]

Christ was without sin, but for your sake God made him share your sin in order that you, in union with him, might share the righteousness of God.[2Co.5:21TEV]

Now when sins have once been forever forgiven and forgotten, there is no need to offer more sacrifices to get rid of them.[Heb.10:18LB]

Who shall separate you from the love of Christ? [Rom. 8:35]

Whoever has God's Son has life.[1Jo.5:12LB]

When you hear what I have to say, and believe in the one who has sent me, you have eternal life. You do not have to face judgment; you have already passed from death into life.[Joh.5:24PME]

God has said, I will never, never fail you nor forsake you. That is why you can say without any doubt or fear, the Lord is my helper and I am not afraid...[Heb. 13:5-6LB]

Jesus said, and lo, I am with you alway, even unto the end of the world.[Mat.28:20]

MIRACLES OF THE LOVE-PLAN

THE MARVEL of a rebirth.
The wonder of a new life.
The comfort of real peace.
The joy of a true friend.
The blessing of good health.

Chapter 19

Five Wonders Of Love

WHEN YOU WELCOME Jesus Christ into your life by faith, there are several miraculous results which can take place in you today, now, because *Now is the accepted time; Now is the day of salvation for you.*[2Co.6:2]

I.

FIRST: You are reborn, re-created, restored to God, made new. You become a child of God.

When you receive Jesus Christ, God gives you the miracle power to become his child.[Joh.1:12]

II.

SECOND: You receive a new spiritual life, the miracle life of God through Jesus Christ in you.

If you are in Christ, you are a new creature. All things become new.[2Co.5:17]

Jesus said, *I am come that you might have life more abundantly.*[Joh.10:10]

III.

THIRD: You receive total peace. Anxiety, hypertension, fear, guilt and condemnation are gone forever.

Jesus said, *Peace I leave with you, my peace I give unto you.*[Joh.14:27]

Being justified by faith, you have peace with God through your Lord Jesus Christ.[Rom.5:1]

IV.

FOURTH: You are restored to friendship, fellowship and life with God, the way you were designed to live on this earth.

Truly your fellowship is with the Father, and with his Son Jesus Christ.[1Jo.1:3]

V.

FIFTH: Your physical body is affected so much by this new inner peace with God that your sicknesses disappear and you experience new physical and mental health.

You will serve the Lord your God, and he will take sickness away from the midst of you.[Exo.23:25]

The Lord forgives all of your iniquities; he heals all of your diseases.[Psa.103:3]

FIVE WONDERS OF LOVE

THE BACHELOR who exploited the girls, and the price of prejudice.

The reason for the cross, and the power of forgiveness.

When dignity and honor are restored, there is no fear or guilt before God.

No crime is punished twice.

Chapter 20

Loaded With Benefits

A SYRIAN TRADER who had lived most of his life in Ghana, attended our great crusade in Accra and heard about God's big love-plan for the first time in his life.

He was a bachelor who exploited African girls to satisfy his sexual passion. He cheated and lied in business and lived an abusive and immoral life.

Finally, he lost his health. He had a paralytic stroke which left the right side of his body useless. In that condition he attended our crusade.

When he heard that God valued human beings so much that He gave His only Son to redeem them to Himself, it was almost too much for that man to comprehend. But he kept coming and listening. Finally it began to dawn upon him that Jesus Christ actually died in his place, having assumed his own guilt and having suffered the legal punishment for all of his sins.

The knowledge that Jesus was crucified to suffer the punishment which he ought to have suffered, caused the man to realize how much God loved and valued him, in spite of the life he had lived.

He comprehended the reason for the cross of Christ; that Jesus bore the penalty of his sins, in his name and in his place so that he could be free of condemnation and guilt before God.

He realized, at last, that God had created human beings in His own image, to walk with Him and to live His lifestyle. God never abandoned His dream to have people close to Him. The glorious change came to him when he realized that Christ had died to save him from the penalty of death, and that His blood was shed to wash away all of the sins he had committed.

No Longer Afraid

As he cried out to God, an indescribable peace came to him and he said, "My fear and guilt were gone. I felt so wonderful and confident in God's presence. I realized that Jesus had already suffered the punishment I merited, and therefore I was free and forgiven. Oh the peace I felt. That was the greatest miracle. I was no longer afraid or guilty. I had peace with God. My sins were gone. I had dignity and honor before God."

He had stood out among the multitude, weeping and thanking God for salvation. Finally when he regained his composure, he realized that all of his paralysis had disappeared. He rubbed the right side of his face that had been twisted and it felt perfect. His right hand, arm and leg were totally restored. The man was saved and healed in the same instant.

He rushed to the platform to tell everyone what had happened.

How he wept as he showed us how his paralysis was gone. But he seemed even more deeply moved as he told us how his guilt and condemnation were replaced by the knowledge that he was pardoned, redeemed to God and restored to dignity. He knew he was forgiven and he was no longer afraid of God.

HOW TO CONFIRM the big love-plan.

It is a wonderful life when God is our friend.

Quality quotations that quell quack questions and quicken quiet confidence.

Our glorious new life to live and to share.

Chapter 21

Jesus Christ Is Your Link

THE MASTER KEY to the divine life within you is to understand and personally relate to what Christ did for you when He died on the cross in your place.

Jesus Christ is your link with God. He removed your judgment by suffering in your place.

Now, all you have to do is to believe. You have the right and freedom to choose to believe.

The moment you decide to believe that Christ's death was on your behalf, then He will come in and live with you forever; you will be saved.

Quality Quotations

I want to share with you some Bible quotations which will confirm to you God's big love-plan.

The first quotation shows you how God wants to have you near Him and how He wants to be near you.

He is a friend that sticks closer than a brother or a sister.[Pro.18:24]

The next quotation reminds us that God's big love-plan is, and has always been based on our confidence in the integrity of His word.

Without faith (if you distrust God) *it is impossible to please God: for anyone who comes to him must believe that he exists, and that he always rewards those who diligently seek him.* [Heb.11:6]

The next group of quotations enumerates the ways Jesus Christ became our personal substitute, assumed our guilt and suffered the penalty of our sins in His death for us on the cross.

Surely Jesus Christ has borne our sicknesses and carried our pains.[Isa.53:4]

Jesus Christ was wounded and bruised for our sins. He was chastised that we might live.[Isa.53:5]

God has laid on Jesus Christ the guilt and sins of everyone of us.[Isa.53:6]

For the transgression of people was Jesus Christ stricken.[Isa.53:8]

He made his soul an offering for (our) *sin.*[Isa.53:10]

Himself (Jesus Christ) *took our infirmities and bare our sicknesses.*[Mat.8:17]

Brought Back as God's Friend

The Bible quotations which follow explain the results we can experience when we understand and believe that Jesus Christ died in our place and endured all of the punishment and condemnation we deserved to suffer.

It was through what God's Son did that he cleared a path for everything to come to him...for Christ's death on the cross has made peace with God for all by his blood.[Col.1:20LB]

This includes you who were once so far away from God...now he has brought you back as his friend. [Col.1:21LB]

He has done this through the death on the cross of his own human body (substituting for you) *and now as a result Christ has brought you into the very presence of God, and you are standing there before him with nothing left against you.*[Col.1:22LB]

The only condition is that you fully believe the truth...convinced of the good news that Jesus died for you.[Col.1:23LB]

Identified With Christ

The following Bible quotations explain how we are personally identified with Jesus Christ in His death, burial and resurrection.

Jesus Christ was wounded for our transgressions. He was bruised for our iniquities.[Isa.53:5]

Our old person is crucified with Jesus Christ so that the body of sin might be destroyed, that from now on we should not serve sin.[Rom.6:6]

We have been planted together in the likeness of his death.[Rom.6:5]

Jesus Christ was raised again for our justification. [Rom.4:25]

God has raised us up together with Christ.[Eph.2:6]

Now if we be dead with Christ, we believe that we shall also live with him.[Rom.6:8] That is not just in heaven, but here and now.

Jesus said, *Lo I am with you alway, even unto the end of the world.*[Mat.28:20]

God says, *I will dwell in them, and walk in them; and I will be their God, and they shall be my people.* [2Co.6:16]

And you…did God make alive together with Jesus Christ.[Eph.2:5-6RSV]

This next Bible verse summarizes these identity facts:

I am crucified with Christ, nevertheless I live; yet not I, but Christ lives in me: and the life which I now live in the flesh, I live by the faith of the Son of God, who loved me, and gave himself for me.[Gal.2:20]

Sharing God's New Life

The next quotations from the Bible will encourage you to always trust in God's big love-plan.

So look upon your old sin nature as dead...and instead be alive to God...through Jesus Christ. Rom.6:11LB

When God the Father, with glorious power, brought Jesus Christ back to life again, you were given his wonderful new life to enjoy...now you share his new life. Rom.6:4-5LB

Whoever believes in Jesus Christ shall not perish, but have eternal life. Joh.3:15

Anyone who believes on the Son has everlasting life. Joh.3:36

Jesus said, *I am come that you might have life... more abundantly.* Joh.10:10

Salvation is not a reward for the good we have done...It is God himself who has made us what we are and given us new lives from Jesus Christ. Eph.2:9-10LB

God gave you a share in the very life of Christ, for he forgave all of your sins, and blotted out the charges proved against you...In this way, God took away Satan's power to accuse you of sin, and He openly displayed to the whole world Christ's triumph at the cross where your sins were taken away. Col.2:13-15LB

So you have everything when you have Christ, and you are filled with God through your union with Christ. Col.2:10

For all things are yours...and you are Christ's; and Christ is God's.[1Co.3:21,23]

Jesus Christ's divine power has given unto us all things that pertain unto life.[2Pe.1:3]

There is given unto us exceeding great and precious promises: that by these we might be partakers of the divine nature.[2Pe.1:4]

JESUS CHRIST IS YOUR LINK

DISCOVER your value.
The basic problem.
Understand God's Integrity.
God desires life for you.
The author of your salvation.
Identify with Christ.
Believe the gospel.

Chapter 22

Know These Facts And Live

BEFORE I GUIDE you in your confession-prayer to receive God's life by accepting Jesus Christ, I will outline for you the seven basic steps for you to take, in order to personally accept God's big love-plan.

FIRST: Believe You Are Valuable as God's Creation

For you are God's workmanship.[Eph.2:10]

God created humankind in his own image[Gen.1:27]*...in the likeness of God.*[Gen.5:1-2]

The Lord made you a little lower than God, (Original Hebrew—God; King James Version—angels), *and crowned you with glory and honor. The Lord gave you dominion over the works of his hands; he put all things under your feet.*[Psa.8:5-6]

SECOND: Know that Distrusting God's Word Is the Original and Basic Problem

And the Lord told Adam and Eve, of every tree of the garden you may freely eat; but of the tree of the knowledge of good and evil, you will not eat of it; for in the day that you eat of it you will surely die.[Gen.2:16-17]

Satan influenced them to distrust God's word. He contradicted God by saying: You will **not** surely die.

Eve took of the fruit and ate it, and gave some to her husband with her; and he ate it.[Gen.3:6]

That was the original sin—distrusting God's word.

THIRD: Understand That Disavowing God's Integrity Results in Death

God said, in the day that you disavow my instructions and eat the fruit I forbade, you will surely die. Gen.2:17

The wages of sin (disavowing the integrity of God's word) *is death.*[Rom.6:23]

Whereas, by one person sin entered into the world, and death by sin; so death passed upon all persons, for that all have sinned.[Rom.5:12]

FOURTH: Believe That God Values You Too Much to Let You Die

For I have no pleasure in the death of anyone who dies, says the Lord: wherefore turn yourself, and live. [Eze.18:32]

God was not willing that any should perish, but that all should come to repentance.[2Pe.3:9]

God so loved the world that he gave his only begotten Son, that whoever believes in him will not perish, but have everlasting life.[Joh.3:16]

But God showed his great love for you by sending Christ to die for you.[Rom.5:8]

FIFTH: Know Why Jesus Came and Died as Your Substitute

The penalty of sin is death.[Rom.6:23] *Death passed upon all persons because all have sinned.*[Rom.5:12] Therefore, we would have to die for our own sins – unless a guiltless substitute would willingly pay our penalty by dying in our place.

Jesus Christ, God's Son *was in all points tempted like as we are, yet without sin.*[Heb.4:15] *He did no sin.* [1Pe.2:24]

Being made perfect, Jesus Christ became the author of eternal salvation.[Heb.5:9]

Jesus Christ bare our sins in his own body, that we, being dead to sins, should live unto righteousness. 1Pe.2:24

God made Jesus Christ who knew no sin to be made sin on our behalf, so that in him we might share the righteousness (or life) *of God.*[2Co.5:21]

SIXTH: Understand the Reason for Christ's Death, Burial and Resurrection

A. When Jesus Christ died, your old life of sin died with Him. Understand and believe that His death was for you.

I have been crucified with Christ.[Gal.2:20]

B. When Jesus Christ was buried, your old life of sin was put away forever. Understand and believe that Christ's burial was on your behalf.

We are buried with Jesus Christ into death.[Rom.6:4]

C. When Jesus Christ was raised from the dead, you were raised up with Him. Understand and believe that His resurrection included you.

God has raised Jesus Christ from the dead and has quickened you together with him, having forgiven you all trespasses.[Col.2:12-13]

D. When Jesus Christ arose in a new life, you arose to walk in that same new life of God. Understand and believe that the new life of Christ can now be imparted to you.

Like as Christ was raised up from the dead by the glory of the Father, even so we also should walk in newness of life.[Rom.6:4]

You are risen with Christ. Christ is your life.[Col.3:1,3]

SEVENTH: Believe the Gospel and Receive Jesus Christ in Person Now

God's big love-plan is based on faith in the integrity of His word and on your right to choose to believe.

Believe on the Lord Jesus Christ and you will be saved.[Acs.16:31]

As many as receive Jesus Christ, he gives to them power to become the children of God.[Joh.1:12]

When He enters your life, He will bring all of His power, health, and miraculous energy with Him. It will be in you. Your dignity and honor are restored.

CHRIST IS your bridge to reunion with God.

You can have dignity again.

You can come home to God and live His original dream.

The confession-prayer that restores you to God's lifestyle.

Chapter 23

God's Reunion With You

BY FAITH, relate yourself to Jesus Christ because He is the way, the bridge, the link, the channel that makes possible your reunion with God and God's reunion with you.

You can now come home to God who created you and values you. You can have dignity again.

God can now come home to you and live in and through you, which was His original dream.

Right now, find a place alone with God. Get on your knees and pray this prayer, out loud.

PRAYER

O GOD, my Father in heaven,

It was You, who wonderfully created me, in Your own image and likeness. My life has great value.

I know I must never destroy what You created. I must never depreciate what You value or despise what You love.

I now know that I am made to walk with You. I was never created for loneliness, sickness, inferiority or guilt.

Without Your life, all that remains is deterioration and death.

O FATHER in heaven, I see now that when You created me, Your dream was to live in me.

You had such love for me that You found a way to save me from deterioration and death.

You gave Your Son, Jesus Christ to come to this world. He was tempted every way possible but He never sinned. He never distrusted Your word or denied Your integrity. He was perfect and without sin.

He became my substitute and assumed the punishment for all of my sins, when He died on the cross.

I do here and now, identify with Jesus Christ.

When He died, my old sinful life died.

When Jesus was buried, my old sinful life was buried.

When Jesus was raised up from the dead in a new life, His new life was offered to me.

You promised that if I received Jesus Christ by faith, Your power would recreate me as Your child and I would have the new Christ-life.

I do, here and now, open my heart and receive Jesus Christ and His new life in me, as my savior and as my lord.

I believe that as I receive Jesus, I receive You, O God.

I do believe that You have now come back to live in me like You originally planned when You created me.

I believe I am saved. You and I are one again because of what Your Son, Jesus, did in my place.

O JESUS, my lord, since You paid the full price for my transgressions, there can never be any further price for me to pay.

Now I am restored to God my Father through Jesus my savior.

DEAR FATHER, all of the abundance You created on this earth is for my blessing. Now, You will supply everything I need, and guide me in obtaining it.

You are my great physician. You know how wonderfully I am made. You live in me now. Your miracle life is the healing life in me now.

There will be no more loneliness, O Lord, because You are my friend. You live in me and I in You.

My sins are punished. They can never be punished again. My debt is paid. No debt can ever be paid twice.

I am saved, here and now.

I believe, and I am free.

Thank You, O Father, and thank You, Lord Jesus.

AMEN.

Chapter 24

Dignity Regained

NOW YOU ARE restored to God, to honor, to dignity, to self-worth.

A miracle life has begun in you.

That is why I wrote this book.

Write to me. Tell me about your new experience and what it means to be part of God's big love-plan. We will reply. We will be friends. Whenever you have a problem or a hurt or a need, we will help you.

We can be partners in helping other people discover God's big love-plan and His wonderful lifestyle.

From the day your letter reaches us, we will be earnestly praying for God's best to come to you and your loved ones.

We will send you a list of other books we have written to help you. One is titled, *The Good Life,* full of terrific power-filled ideas to help you experience life's best.

We have recorded some remarkable cassette albums which can be a great help and inspiration to you.

Jesus made a wonderful promise.

If you will confess me before people, I will confess you before my Father in heaven.[Mat.10:32]

The finest way to say thanks to God for His big love-plan is to share this happy information with others.

THE *MISSION* OF CHRISTIANITY

OSBORN MINISTRY REVIEW

THE GLOBAL MISSION of Christianity is to witness of Christ and of His resurrection to *the entire world*—to *every creature.* (See Mk.16:15)

The Apostle Paul said, …*"Everyone who calls on the name of the Lord will be saved."* Rom.10:13

T.L. and Daisy Osborn shared a worldwide ministry together for over five decades, before her demise in 1995. T.L. continued his global ministry to multitudes until his passing in 2013.

The Osborn daughter, Dr. LaDonna, is the President and CEO of Osborn Ministries International, the ministry founded by her parents in 1949. Her ministry touches practically every continent via face-to-face ministry, through public mass evangelism *Festivals of Faith and Miracles* and trans-evangelical *Gospel Seminars,* and a variety of internet ministry platforms.

Dr. LaDonna's visionary leadership and expertise are making possible the expansion of this ministry in nations around the world. Learn more about the Osborn global outreaches through their official website at ***osborn.org***.

Drs. T.L., Daisy and LaDonna Osborn have reached millions for Christ in over a hundred nations during more than six decades already. This ministry-brief is included here to inspire young believers that they, too, can carry the *gospel torch into all the world.*(See Mk.16:15)

Mass Miracle Evangelism

Tommy Lee Osborn and Daisy Marie Washburn were married in Los Banos, California in 1942, at the ages of 17 and 18. In 1945 they went to India as missionaries but were unable to convince the people of these ancient religions—Muslims and Hindus—about Christ. They had not yet discovered the truths about healing miracles. They returned to the USA dismayed and disheartened—but not dissuaded.

Soon after their demoralizing return home, the Lord appeared to them both, at different times, as they searched for the answer to their dilemma.

- They began to discover the Bible truths that create faith for biblical miracles.
- They had learned in India that for people of non-Christian nations to believe the gospel, they must witness miracle proof that Jesus Christ is alive today.

- They discovered that signs, miracles and wonders are essential to convincing *non*-Christian nations about the gospel.

> Jesus was...***accredited by God*** *to you by* ***miracles, wonders*** *and* **signs**, *which God did among you through him, as you yourselves know* (emphasis added).Ac.2:22

These dynamic truths created in their spirits fresh faith in God's Word. With this new lease on life and having discovered the scriptural facts about miracles they, along with their children, *re*-launched their soulwinning saga in 1949—this time in the Caribbean island-nation of Jamaica.

During thirteen weeks of ministry there, hundreds of biblical miracles confirmed their preaching.

- Over a hundred deaf-mutes were healed;
- Over ninety totally blind people received sight;
- Hundreds of crippled, paralyzed and lame people were restored;
- Most important of all, *nearly ten thousand souls received Jesus Christ as their Savior.*

That success motivated their new global ministry, proclaiming the gospel to multitudes. In the era when developing nations were mostly *colonized* by European governments, the Osborns pioneered the concept of *Mass Miracle Evangelism.* Such methods had not been witnessed since the epoch of the Early

Church. T.L. and Daisy addressed audiences of tens of thousands throughout the dangerous years of *nationalism* when the awakening of many developing nations was repulsing foreign political domination.

Their example inspired national men and women, globally, to arise from their restrictive past, and to become leading gospel messengers and church builders in the unevangelized nations of the world. Many of them are numbered among the most distinguished and successful Christian leaders today.

The largest churches in the world are no longer in America or Europe. Anointed and talented national pastors are raising them up. Single churches in Africa seat 50,000 plus people. To God be the glory.

Drs. T.L. and Daisy's partial testimony is recorded for posterity in their 512 page unique Memorial Edition pictorial, THE GOSPEL ACCORDING TO T.L. AND DAISY.

Global Evangelism Concepts

During T.L. and Daisy's unprecedented years as an evangelism team, they inaugurated numerous programs to reach the unreached. Their concept of *National Missionary Assistance* resulted in them sponsoring over 30,000 national preachers as full time missionaries to unevangelized tribes and villages where new, self-supporting churches became established globally.

The Osborn literature is published in more than 130 languages. Their DocuMiracle crusade films, audio and video CDs and DVDs are produced in over 70 languages and their digital productions (including Bible courses) are circulated around the world.

They have provided airlifts and huge shipments of literature and of soulwinning tools for gospel ministries abroad. They have furnished scores of four-wheel drive vehicles equipped with films, projectors, screens, generators, public-address systems, audiocassettes and cassette players, plus literature for reaching the unreached.

Publishing The Gospel

Dr. Daisy's five major books are *pacesetters* in Christian literature for women—*unique examples of **inclusive** language that consistently addresses both men and women.*

Dr. T.L. has authored over 20 major books. He wrote his first, HEALING THE SICK, during their mission to Jamaica in 1950. Now in its 46th edition, it is a global favorite, used as a Bible School text book in many nations.

The publisher calls HEALING THE SICK—*A Living Classic*—a faith-building best seller since 1950.

Over a million copies are in print, circulating healing truth throughout the world.

Dr. LaDonna's book, GOD'S BIG PICTURE is published in scores of languages and is heralded globally as the single most important book to make clear the story of the Bible, from Genesis to Revelation. Through this book, people discover their place in God's plan.

Some of her other books, such as CHAOS OF MIRACLES, JESUS IS TOUCHING SOSHANGUVE and UNKNOWN BUT NOT FORGOTTEN are modern day accounts of Christ's ministry in action through her as she ministers the gospel among some of the world's unreached masses.

The history of the Osborn Ministries International is also recorded in their unique and historical 24-volume *Encyclo-Biographical Anthology*. It contains more than 23,000 pages, 30,946 photos, 636 *Faith Digest* magazines, 2,024 pages of personal hand-written diary notes, 1,011 pages of Osborns' news letters, 1,062 pages of unpublished historical data about their world ministry, 2,516 world mission reports, and 6,113 Christian ministry reports.

These 24 giant tomes span over six feet of shelf space and have taken their place in the archives and libraries of institutions of higher learning around the world, including such renowned universities and libraries as: University of Cambridge, Cambridge, England; University of Oxford,

Oxford, England; Asbury Theological Seminary, Wilmore, USA; British Library, London, England; Central Bible College, Springfield, USA; Christ for the Nations, Dallas, USA; Fuller Theological Seminary, Pasadena, USA; Messenger College, Joplin, USA; National Library, Sofia, Bulgaria; Oral Roberts University, Tulsa, USA; Ramkhamhaeng University, Bangkok, Thailand; Regent University, Virginia Beach, USA; Universidad Interamericana de Puerto Rico, Ponce, Puerto Rico; Université de Cocody, Abidjan, Ivory Coast; University of Ghana, Legon-Accra, Ghana; Université de Kinshasa, Kinshasa, Democratic Republic of the Congo; Université de Lomé, Lomé, Togo; University of Nairobi, Nairobi, Kenya; University of Maseno, Maseno, Kenya; Université Marien Ngouabi, Brazzaville, Congo; Université Omar Bongo, Libreville, Gabon; University of Wales, Bangor, Wales; Vernadsky National Library, Kiev, Ukraine; Word of Life, Uppsala, Sweden; (plus many more), and the archives of many leading denominational headquarters.

Their Global Saga

Dr. LaDonna C. Osborn continues to enlarge the scope of the Osborn ministries of evangelism and training to nearly every continent as she carries the *torch of the gospel* into this century's new frontiers.

Like the Apostle Paul, Dr. LaDonna says:

> ***I am not ashamed of the gospel, because it is the power of God that brings salvation to everyone who believes...*** Rom.1:16

She believes that:

*The World is the **Heart** of the Church,*
*The Church is the **Hope** of the World.*

She contends that:

Without the *World,* the *Church is **meaningless*** –
Without the *Church,* the *World is **hopeless**.*

Colonialism
Nationalism
Globalism/Evangelism

Dr. LaDonna C. Osborn knows the ministry of World Evangelism. Since childhood, she has lived on the front lines of global SOULWINNING—from the days of *colonialism,* through the turbulent years of *nationalism,* and into this century of *globalism, mass evangelism* and *national* and *international Church growth.*

She holds forth these simple truths:

1. The Bible is as valid today as it ever was;

2. The divine calling for every believer is to witness of Christ to the unconverted;

3. Every soul won to Christ can become His representative; and

4. Miracles, signs and wonders are what distinguish Christianity from being just another philosophical religion.

To demonstrate these biblical issues is the essence of the global *MISSION of Christianity.*

Just as with the Apostle Paul, Dr. LaDonna states:

> *...the task the Lord Jesus has given me – the task of testifying to the good news of God's grace.*[Ac.20:24] *...we can preach the gospel in the regions beyond...*[2Cor.10:16]

- The Osborns' continuing passion:

  To express and propagate the gospel of Jesus Christ to all people throughout the world.

- Their tenet for action:

  No one deserves to hear the gospel repeatedly before everyone has heard it at least once.

- Their motto:

  ***One Way—Jesus;
One Job—Evangelism.***

- Their guiding principle:

  Every Christian believer—a witness for Christ.

Their witness is expressed best by the words of the Apostle John:

> *who testifies to everything he saw – that is, the word of God and the testimony of Jesus Christ.* [Rev.1:2] We testify *...of these things, and wrote these things; and we know that* (our) *...testimony is true* (emphasis added). [Jn. 21:24 NKJV]

ACTION Ideas

You have not chosen me but I have chosen you, and ordained you, that you should go and bring forth fruit, and that your fruit should remain: that whatever you shall ask of the Father in my name, he may give it you. Joh.15:16

ACTION Results

....

....

....

....

....

....

....

....

....

....

....

....

....

....

....

....

....

....

....

....

....

....

....

....

....

As many as received Jesus Christ, to them he gave power to become the children of God, even to them that believe on his name. Joh.1:12

GLOBAL PUBLISHER

OSBORN PUBLICATIONS
P.O. Box 10
Tulsa, OK 74102 USA

✧✧✧

FRENCH DISTRIBUTOR

ÉDITIONS
MINISTÈRES MULTILINGUES
909, Boul. Roland-Therrien
Longueuil, Québec J4J 4L3 Canada

✧✧✧

GERMAN PUBLISHER

SHALOM – VERLAG
Pachlinger Strrasse 10
D-93486 Runding, CHAM, Germany

✧✧✧

PORTUGUESE PUBLISHER

GRACA EDITORIAL
Caixa Postal 1815
Rio de Janiero–RJ–20001, Brazil

✧✧✧

SPANISH PUBLISHER

LIBROS DESAFIO, Apdo. 29724
Bogota, Colombia

www.osborn.org